Growing Up
IN THE
PIEDMONT TRIAD
BOOMER MEMORIES FROM
KRISPY KREME TO COCA-COLA PARTIES

ALICE E. SINK

THE
History
PRESS

Published by The History Press
Charleston, SC 29403
www.historypress.net

Cover image courtesy of Forsyth County Public Library Photograph Collection. Back cover
kitchen image courtesy of Library of Congress.

First published 2012

ISBN 978.1.54023.267.0

Library of Congress CIP data applied for

In loving memory of the deceased members of Lexington Senior High School, class of 1958: Martha Biesecker, David Bullaboy, Diane Dickerson, Barbara Garren, Martha Grayson, Jimmy Haire, Martha Hathcock, Anita Hedrick, Jean Hedrick, Carol Hunt, Jerry Hunt, Ralph Jones, Rayvon Jones, Gayle Koontz, Bob Lee, Bob Leonard, Larry Leonard, Ollie Loggins, Sylvia McLean, Donese Owens, Tommy Phillips, Charles Russell, Wayne Sechler, Don Sexton, Jerry Stiles, Peggy Tussey and Lynn Wall.

Contents

Introduction

G rowing up in the Piedmont Triad of North Carolina from 1940 to 1960 was not as peaceful, calm and serene as some folks might think. There were crimes, prejudices, polio epidemics and, of course, World War II. But there were good times, too. The television shows, popular songs and various school events, as well as the camaraderie enjoyed as we involved ourselves in civic, social and religious organizations, made our innocent lives enjoyable.

Twelve counties make up the Piedmont Triad: Alamance, Caswell, Davidson, Davie, Forsyth, Guilford, Montgomery, Randolph, Rockingham, Stokes, Surry and Yadkin.

The Piedmont Triad—or Triad, as the area is often called—consists of the area within and surrounding the three major cities of Greensboro, Winston-Salem and High Point. Triad cities with more than ten thousand people in population include Archdale, Asheboro, Burlington, Clemmons, Eden, Graham, Kernersville, Lewisville, Lexington, Mebane, Mount Airy, Reidsville, Summerfield and Thomasville.

Other Triad municipalities under ten thousand in population include Alamance, Bermuda Run, Bethania, Boonville, Cooleemee, Danbury, Denton, Dobson, East Bend, Elkin, Elon, Franklinville, Gibsonville, Glen Raven, Green Level, Haw River, Jamestown, Jonesville, King, Liberty, Madison, Mayodan, Midway, Mocksville, Oak Ridge, Ossipee, Pleasant Garden, Ramseur, Randleman, Rural Hall, Saxapahaw, Seagrove, Sedalia, Staley, Stokesdale, Stoneville, Swepsonville, Tobaccoville,

Trinity, Walkertown, Wallburg, Walnut Cove, Welcome, Wentworth, Whitsett and Yadkinville.

No matter where one grew up in one of these areas, children and young people often experienced the same joys and sorrows. The city or town or municipality in the Piedmont Triad sometimes varied only in size and scheduled events. Many things stayed about the same.

The celebrity images are courtesy of the Library of Congress and various Internet sources. The author's antique photographs included in the book were made with her old Brownie camera—you know, the one with film where you had to concentrate on every shot and every frame because you paid for twenty-four exposures, and there were no do-overs. Gone are the days of hearing the film rewind into its casing, transporting it to a photo lab and patiently waiting to find out how amateurish your snapshots looked.

PART I

Entertainment

EARLY BLACK-AND-WHITE TELEVISION, SOAPS AND TEST PATTERNS

If a Piedmont Triad family were lucky enough to own one of the first black-and-white television sets, they may have purchased a three-color plastic sheet that sat on the screen in order to magically turn black-and-white into color. It took three minutes for the TV to warm up. The station went off the air at midnight after playing the national anthem and reciting a poem about God. A TV test pattern came on after signoff and stayed there until two, maybe three o'clock. Channels

Family members watching the black-and-white twenty-one-inch television set in the den of their home. *Courtesy of author.*

came back on the air at about 6:00 a.m., and those usually broadcast locally produced news and farm shows, featuring local people.

In 1952, a Piedmont Triad family could purchase the Balfour, a twenty-one-inch TV/radio/phonograph—three gifts in one set. Features included Zenith TV, powered by the amazing "KI-53" chassis, plus the sensational Cobra-Magic 78 RPM—including the new 16 RPM Complete FM/AM radio—all in a beautiful, ultramodern blonde cabinet. The cost was $725.

Television soap operas captured the attention of many homemakers. Following was the lineup for May 5, 1955:

- 10:30—WAY OF THE WORLD—*First day home for Cynthia and Walt after their honeymoon. Her brother Fred blackmails $50 out of her to bet on a horse and to "keep quiet about those calls from New York." Claire drops in, warns Walt, "You'll never find emotional security with Cynthia. She's an opportunist."*

- 12:00 noon—VALIANT LADY—*Helen wishes Chris happy birthday. For a few seconds they're actually happy, until he opens her present. She: "What's the matter?" He: "Linda used to give me a pipe every birthday. But, of course you had no way of knowing." In mental hospital, Linda begins to recover her mind, remembers his name was Chris, remembers it's his birthday, remembers about the pipes, begs the doctor to let her see Chris. Organ music swells up, underlining Chris' gathering problems: What will he do with two women who love and need him—and with all those pipes?*

- 12:30—SEARCH FOR TOMORROW—*Scene: A hospital. Mrs. Barron plans to marry Arthur Tate, who is recovering from heart surgery, just as soon as he can "walk the length of the corridor." They'll be married in a room at the end of the corridor. The doctor worries and comments: "Anyone of us can walk out of this hospital and be struck by a car." Organ music comes up with doctor still fretting: "Tate can get well. But who knows that will happen tomorrow."*

Throughout its entire thirty-five-year run, *Search's* title sequence featured a shot of clouds floating through the sky. Years later, the only noticeable change was the slightly altered "s" in "search" upon switching to color. In late 1981, it switched to a glitzy new videotaped opening sequence beginning with a shot of a seagull flying over the ocean, followed by a helicopter shot of the clouds in the midday sky. In the show's final months, the titles featured a montage of cast clips, bookended with sky shots. The show's initial sponsor was Procter & Gamble, the makers of Joy dishwashing liquid and Spic and Span household cleaner.

Piedmont Triad TV viewers tuned in to view Dr. Joyce Brothers—American psychologist, television personality and advice columnist—gain fame in late 1955 by winning the *$64,000 Question* game show, on which she appeared as an expert in the subject area of boxing. A voracious reader, she had studied every reference book about boxing that she could find. She later told reporters that "it was thanks to her good memory that assimilated so much material and answered even the most difficult questions."

Interestingly, the first time a man and woman were shown in bed together on primetime TV was the show *Mary Kay and Johnny.* Starring real-life married couple Mary Kay Stearns and Johnny Stearns, the show debuted in 1947. The couple created and wrote all the scripts. The program was broadcast live, most of the action taking place on a set representing the New York City apartment of the title characters, a young married couple. This show was also the first television series to show a woman's pregnancy on television. In 1948, Mary Kay became pregnant. After unsuccessfully trying to hide it, the show's producers wrote her pregnancy into the show. On December 31, 1948, the Stearnses' son, Christopher, less than one month old, appeared on the show and became a character.

Drooling Over Favorite Movie Stars

Ann Southern and Lucille Ball

One of the headlines for an October 30, 1957 article read, "Ann Southern to Leave TV for New Film with Lucille Ball." The article that followed informed readers that a movie starring Southern and Ball would obviously prove to be hilarious. Ann Southern, former star of the television show *Private Secretary*, made this statement when interviewed by columnist Bob Thomas: "Lucy and I hit it off real good, and we may do the movie together. Strangely enough we had never worked together before, though we were both at MGM at the same time."

Southern further stated that she definitely would not give up television because she had another series that she had been working on for two years. "It's about firemen, and I've spent hours at firehouses doing research. It's the only exciting kind of work that hasn't been done in a TV series, and it has great possibilities. Firemen don't just put out fires; you find them everywhere—at

Lucille Ball, of the popular TV show *I Love Lucy*, joined Ann Southern of *Private Secretary* in a hilarious new movie. *Courtesy of doctormacro.com.*

drowning, riots, auto crashes, disasters, and so forth." Southern concluded her interview by emphasizing, "No more *Private Secretary!*"

Hollywood news found its way to Piedmont Triad newspapers. Readers liked to keep up with events involving their favorite stars.

Smiling June Allyson and Dick Powell said that their separation rumors were true. *Courtesy of Wikimedia Commons.*

Dick Powell and June Allyson

One interesting article informed fans that June Allyson was returning to Hollywood from New York, but Dick Powell said that he supposed that the separation rumors would start all over again. "I may go pheasant hunting in South Dakota," he said. "What am I supposed to do? Sit here and twiddle my thumbs?" Dick went on a flight to visit his alma mater, the University of Arkansas.

Veronica Lake

This Hollywood item got the attention of movie fans: "If Veronica Lake's mama meant to imply in her support suit that the famed peek-a-boo bob girl makes $4,500 a week every week in the year, she is misinformed. Veronica's contract with Paramount is for two pictures a year, with a 10-week guarantee on each picture. And she gets paid only when she is working. What's more, due to the baby, she has made only one picture at Paramount this year."

Young girls—and sometimes boys—growing up in the Piedmont Triad loved to play Hollywood hopscotch. Squares were drawn on the sidewalk. The first player hopped on one foot from beginning to end and then was awarded the honor of putting a movie star's initials in one of the squares. If her opponent could correctly guess the name of the celebrity, she earned the right to go next.

MOVIE OF INTEREST THROUGHOUT THE PIEDMONT TRIAD

In 1956, Piedmont Triad citizens literally flocked to the Winston Theatre in downtown Winston-Salem to see the movie *Written on the Wind*, an American drama directed by Douglas Sirk. It starred Rock Hudson, Lauren Bacall, Robert Stack and Dorothy Malone. The screenplay by George Zuckerman was based on Robert Wilder's 1945 novel of the same name, "a thinly disguised account of the real-life scandal involving torch singer Libby Holman and her husband, tobacco heir Zachary Smith Reynolds." Zuckerman shifted the locale from North Carolina to Texas, made the source of the family wealth oil rather than tobacco and changed all the characters' names.

The plot was about a self-destructive, alcoholic nymphomaniac named Marylee and her insecure, alcoholic playboy brother, Kyle, the children of Texas oil baron Jasper Hadley. Spoiled by their inherited wealth and crippled by their personal demons, neither is able to sustain a personal relationship. Problems ensue after Kyle's impulsive marriage to New York City executive secretary Lucy Moore, who becomes a steadying influence to his life through the first few months after they meet. Kyle resumes drinking after being unsuccessful in fathering a baby. He turns against his childhood friend, Marylee's longtime infatuation, Mitch Wayne, a geologist for the oil company. Kyle's anger and depression grow after the death of his father, who admired Mitch but was disgusted with the behavior of his two heirs.

Mitch is secretly in love with Lucy. He keeps these feelings private until Kyle, having been diagnosed with a low sperm count, physically assaults Lucy when she announces her pregnancy, wrongly assuming it to be the result of adultery with Mitch. Lucy's fall results in a miscarriage. Mitch vows to leave town with her as soon as she's well enough to travel. Upon his return, a drunken Kyle recovers a hidden pistol and intends to shoot Mitch. Marylee struggles with her brother for the weapon, but it accidentally fires, killing him.

Repeatedly spurned by the man she claims to love, a spiteful Marylee threatens to implicate Mitch in Kyle's death. At the inquest, she first testifies that he killed her sibling. But she tearfully redeems herself at the last second by admitting the truth. Mitch and Lucy depart, leaving Marylee to mourn the death of her brother and run the company alone.

Bosley Crowther, who reviewed the movie for the *New York Times*, wrote, "The trouble with this romantic picture…is that nothing really happens, the complications within the characters are never clear and the sloppy, self-pitying fellow at the center of the whole thing is a bore." *TV Guide* described the film as "the ultimate in lush melodrama, Douglas Sirk's finest directorial effort," and as "one of the most notable critiques of the American family ever made."

Regardless of the varying reviews, this was probably the first movie in a long time where the audience stood and applauded as the credits ran.

In general, movie stars kissed with their mouths shut. There were no movie ratings yet because all movies were responsibly produced for everyone to enjoy, without profanity or violence or most anything offensive.

SOUGHT-AFTER MAGAZINES FEATURING HOLLYWOOD STARS

In the '50s, practically every newsstand in the Piedmont Triad displayed at least one popular "movie star" magazine. In December 1953, Hugh Hefner published the first edition of *Playboy*. Marilyn Monroe was featured. When asked what she had on during the photo shoot, she replied, "the radio." Bettie Page was the Playmate of the Month in January 1955. *Playboy* was the first magazine featuring nude glamour photography targeted at the mainstream consumer. The British Queen of Curves in the 1950s and early '60s was Pamela Green. Harrison Marks, on the encouragement of Green, took up glamour photography, and they published the pinup magazine *Kamera* together in 1957. In England, the earliest use of the word "glamour" as a euphemism for nude modeling or photography is attributed to Marks's publicity material in the 1950s.

Of course, kids growing up in the Piedmont Triad of North Carolina never had public access to these magazines. They were all kept "behind the counter" at newsstands or hotel lobbies. However, many probably dug into their male relatives' stashes when those adults were not aware.

The October 1955 copy of *Photoplay* included pictures and stories about Doris Day, Grace Kelly, Janet Leigh and Mitzi Gaynor. In addition, articles in the magazine bore enticing titles such as "Pinups Stage a Manhunt," "Vote Today—Choose Your Stars" and "Rory Calhoun—Love in the Shadow of Fear."

Movieland, Modern Screen and *Screen World* promised true stories that were "fluffy and frothy," new photographs of the stars and Hollywood gossip.

Hedda Hopper wrote many of the articles featuring top movie stars. In April 1952, she teased the reading public with a cover title that read, "The Truth about the Kathryn Grayson–Mario Lonza Feud." Cover titles encouraged star worship—especially ones like "Sex and Sin in Hollywood," "Date Bait for Fess Parker" and "Robert Mitchum—The Man Who Dared to Sue."

Teenage girls often bought one monthly magazine, read it and exchanged with friends. With a limited magazine-buying budget, young ladies had access to all the news and gossip of Hollywood. Boys weren't particularly interested in many magazines, except *National Geographic*, which sometimes featured faraway women with bared breasts.

AMOS 'N' ANDY AND OTHER POPULAR RADIO SHOWS

In the early 1950s, many classic radio shows were on the air. Live music shows and soap operas were the last two formats to survive. Some of the most popular shows were *Arthur Godfrey Time, The Eddie Cantor Show, Our Miss Brooks, Amos 'n' Andy, Lucky Strike Hit Parade, The Grand Ole Opry, Howdy Doody, Mr. Keen, Tracer of Lost Persons* and *The Lone Ranger*. Today, many of those early listeners can still hum the music that introduced the shows. *Guiding Light* was the longest-running daytime drama; it moved from radio to TV in 1952.

MUSIC AND DANCES: REMEMBER THE TWIST?

During the early 1950s, the big bands and crooners of the previous decade were still popular. Vocal groups specialized in close harmonies and upbeat doo-wop music. Toward the end of the decade, calypso and lounge music went hand in hand with the exotic new Tiki lifestyle. Classical jazz evolved into progressive and cool jazz. Blues music was sanitized for white audiences and eventually became the basis for rock-and-roll.

Country music entered the mainstream. The use of electric guitars gave it a modern sound, and a blurring of the lines between country, rock and blues meant that people from all walks of life could enjoy it. In the early '50s, a folk revival was ready to begin, but it was suppressed when folk singers were harassed and blacklisted during the McCarthy communist witch hunts. In 1958, the folk movement enjoyed a rebirth that lasted into the 1960s. In 1956, rock music gained a wider audience when Bill Haley's "Rock Around the Clock" was featured in the movie *The Blackboard Jungle*.

The Twist, a dance done by swiveling the hips, became a Piedmont Triad craze in the late '50s. No one is quite sure who actually started swiveling their hips in this manner. Some say it might have been part of an African dance brought to the United States during the era of slavery. Musician Hank Ballard made the dance popular. He wrote and recorded the song "The Twist" after seeing some people twisting their hips while dancing. "The Twist" was first released on the b-side of Ballard's single "Teardrops on Your Letter" in 1958. One source indicates that Hank Ballard and the Midnighters had a reputation for being a risqué band (many of their songs featured explicit lyrics).

It would take another singer, though, to take "The Twist" to number one on the charts. That singer was Chubby Checker, who created his own version of "The Twist":

Come on baby let's do the twist
Come on baby let's do the twist
Take me by my little hand and go like this
Ee-oh twist baby baby twist
Oooh-yeah just like this
Come on little miss and do the twist

My daddy is sleepin' and mama ain't around
Yeah daddy is sleepin' and mama ain't around
We're gonna twisty twisty twisty
'Till we turn the house down
Come on and twist yeah baby twist
Oooh-yeah just like this
Come on little miss and do the twist

Yeah you should see my little Sis
You should see my my little Sis
She really knows how to rock
She knows how to twist
Come on and twist yeah baby twist
Oooh-yeah just like this
Come on little miss and do the twist
Yeah rock on now
Yeah twist on now
Twist.

Chubby Checker sang and danced his version of "The Twist" on Dick Clark's Saturday night program, *The Dick Clark Show.* The song quickly hit number one on the charts, and the dance swept around the world. The Twist was usually done with a partner, although no touching was involved. Some describe it as if you are pretending to stamp out a fallen cigarette or dry your back with a towel. The dance was so popular that it inspired additional dances, such as the Mashed Potato, the Swim and the Funky Chicken.

In 1958, Ross Bagdasarian (using the stage name David Seville) had a major hit with the novelty song "Witch Doctor." The chorus featured nonsense words sung in a comical voice created by speeding up the audiotape.

Popular dances in the 1950s also included the Bop, Stroll, Madison, Cha-Cha, Hand Jive and Jitterbug. For teens, dances were less about romance and more about having fun with friends. Square dancing became popular in the '50s, and teen birthday parties involved renting the Lion's Den, engaging a talented square dance "caller" and serving Cokes and potato chips for refreshments.

The oldest recording format in use was the 78 RPM record. These discs were ten inches wide, made of shellac and contained four minutes of music per side. Longer musical selections and artist compilations were packaged in attractive boxes containing four to six records each. They were called "albums" because the record sleeves folded out like the pages of a book. Columbia stopped making 78s in 1955, and RCA Victor stopped making them in 1958.

Also known as "LPs," these large vinyl discs were introduced in 1948. They were played at $33\frac{1}{3}$ RPM and featured microgroove technology, which resulted in an extended playback time of twenty-three minutes per side. LPs were originally offered in both ten-inch and twelve-inch formats, but the smaller size proved unpopular and was phased out in the mid-1950s.

Introduced in 1949, 45 **RPM** records were seven inches wide and made of durable vinyl plastic. Like the 78s that came before, 45 **RPM** records were perfect for short popular tunes.

Jukeboxes, first produced in the 1920s, reached the height of their popularity in the 1950s. The cost was five songs for a quarter!

POPULAR TELEVISION SHOWS THROUGHOUT THE PIEDMONT TRIAD

In 1953, daily newspapers ran television scheduling for WFMY-TV Channel 2 and WBTV Channel 3. Those were the only two channels available, so viewers could choose one or the other. Popular nighttime programs on Channel 2 included *The Lone Ranger, Douglas Edwards News, 4-Star Playhouse, The Garry Moore Show* and *Strike It Rich*. Channel 3 aired *The Groucho Marx Show, Lux Theatre, Dangerous Assignment* and *Art Linkletter*.

Julius Henry "Groucho" Marx was an American comedian and film and television star who was known as the master of quick wit and widely considered one of the best comedians of the era. His rapid-fire, often impromptu delivery of innuendo-laden language earned him many admirers and imitators. His exaggerated stooped posture, glasses, cigar and thick greasepaint mustache and eyebrows resulted in the creation of one of the world's most recognizable novelty disguises, known as "Groucho glasses."

The first incarnation of *The Garry Moore Show* began in June 1950 as a Monday-through-Friday thirty-minute evening series. The show had changed to a once-weekly, one-hour format by August. In the fall of 1950, CBS rescheduled the show each weekday in the afternoon, and it ran in this format until mid-1958. The series featured a relaxed and flexible combination of comedy, skits, monologues, singing and interaction with the studio audience.

COMIC STRIPS—NEVER ON SUNDAYS

Sunday comic strips entertained both young and old during the 1950s. Kids loved *Peanuts*, drawn by Charles Schulz. Another favorite was *Blondie*, where Dagwood slept in his chair with Zs coming from his mouth while

Charles Schulz drew the popular comic strip *Peanuts*, adored by both kids and adults. *Courtesy of Wikimedia Commons.*

Blondie painted his toenails. Then there was brave *Popeye* and his escapades with Wimpy, Swee'pea and Oscar. *Secret Agent X-9* appealed to young male readers, who admired "Dressy" Pooma, exiled from the United States, and his weekly visit from the local police. *Snuffy Smith*, an all-time, long-running favorite, featured Snuffy, with the "bodacious trial" of Judge Potter trying Snuffy as a chicken thief.

Next came *Ozark Ike*, with Bubbuh Bean and Dinah. *Etta Kett* was also read and enjoyed, as was *Buz Sawyer*, who was stranded on a shipwrecked island without fresh water or fire. One of the five-star cartoons was *Roy Rogers*, whose hero led a fight to halt the fire sweeping across Shasta Valley.

While many Piedmont Triad children were not allowed to engage in play or games on Sunday afternoons, others were not permitted to read the "funnies."

STOCK CAR RACES AT BOWMAN GRAY STADIUM

The first Grand National (now Sprint Cup) Series event took place in 1958, and it was won by Bob Welborn. Other winners include Glen Wood, Rex

White, David Pearson, Richard Petty, Bobby Allison, Junior Johnson and Marvin Panch. The NASCAR Grand National Series first raced at Bowman Gray Stadium, a NASCAR-sanctioned one-fourth-mile asphalt flat oval short track located in Winston-Salem, North Carolina. It is one of stock car racing's most legendary venues and is referred to as "NASCAR's longest-running racetrack."

A stock car, in the original sense of the term, described an automobile that had not been modified from its original factory configuration. Later, the term came to mean any production-based automobile used in racing. This term is used to differentiate such a car from a "race car," a special, custom-built car designed only for racing purposes.

In 1957, the following notable events happened in the sport:

The Automobile Manufacturers Association (AMA) banned manufacturers from using race wins in their advertising and giving direct support to race teams, as they felt it led to reckless street racing. This forced manufacturers to become creative in producing race parts to help racers win. Race teams were often caught trying to use factory produced racing parts that were not really available to the public, though many parts passed muster by being labeled as heavy-duty "Police" parts. Car manufacturers wanted to appear compliant with the ban, but they also wanted to win.

NASCAR tracks at the time were mainly dirt tracks with modest barriers, and during the 1957 season a Mercury Monterey crashed into the crowd. This killed many spectators and resulted in a serious overhaul of the safety rules which in turn prompted the building of larger more modern tracks. Also in 1957, Chevrolet sold enough of their new fuel injected engines to the public in order to make them available for racing, but Bill France immediately banned fuel injection and superchargers from NASCAR before they could race. However, even without official factory support or the use of fuel injection, Buck Baker won in 1957 driving a small-block V-8 Chevrolet Bel-Air.

The NASCAR Grand National Series hosted a total of twenty-nine Grand National races up to 1971. Some of the best NASCAR drivers at that time were Lee Petty, Richard Petty, Bobby Allison, Ralph Earnhardt and Ned Jarrett.

SATURDAY SHOPPING AT THE DIME STORE

Throughout the Piedmont Triad during the '40s and '50s, dime stores—or "five-and-dimes" as they were sometimes called—were familiar sights in most downtown business areas. According to one observer, "Woolworth's was the original and dominant dime store chain. In the first half of the twentieth century, virtually every town and city…featured a Woolworth's; it was the first place many people went to look for basic merchandise of all sorts."

The downtown S.H. Kress & Company in Greensboro, North Carolina, is an excellent example. This chain used elaborate exterior details including coats of arms, metalwork and inlaid artistic flourishes on the keystone sand corners. The Winston-Salem Kress dime store at the corner of Fourth and Liberty Streets witnessed some of the earliest civil rights demonstrations in the South when Carol Matthews was inspired by the sit-in in Greensboro.

These events, although extremely important in the annals of history, probably had little to do with our Piedmont Triad experiences growing up. To a kid in the '40s and '50s, the dime store was a special afternoon place where we could window-shop, browse through all the interesting merchandise and spend our dime allowances. It was a peaceful spot that carried the newest comic books and wonderful aromas of popcorn, hot peanuts and Cherry Cokes. Dime stores were also mysterious havens that held costume jewelry that looked like real diamonds. The wooden floors were perfect if we chose to roller-skate inside, and nobody ever told us to leave. This is where we bought our toys, paper dolls and playing cards. A dime would buy Adams Black Jack chewing gum, which was the first chewing gum to be offered in sticks as we know them today. Black Jack has been brought back to the market as a limited-edition nostalgia product at seventy-five cents per pack. Also for a dime, '50s kids could buy looms for weaving potholders, jigsaw puzzles, craft patterns and coloring books. Or we just spent our dimes on galloping rides on the mechanical horse.

While our mothers purchased old-fashioned wire pants stretchers that put creases in trousers, dishcloths, dress patterns or heart-shaped bottles of Blue Waltz perfume, kids could spend almost the entire Saturday afternoon looking and wishing. What should we buy? A water-filled bird whistle? A windup toy of a cat that chased a ball? Orange slices from the glass-frosted candy case? We always spent our weekly dimes, which the clerk rang up on the manual cash register. We left happy and looking forward to more grown-up days when we could purchase a coveted beaded hairnet.

Batter Up!

Summer evening professional baseball games drew families to Holt-Moffitt Field to watch the Lexington Indians, ranking high in North Carolina State League standing, battle the Thomasville Hi-Toms. The big contest between these two Piedmont Triad opponents was always exciting. The stadium filled to capacity, the floodlights shone and the aroma of hot dogs, chili and onions drifted from the concession stand. After everyone stood reverently for the national anthem, the booming declaration came over the intercom: "Play ball!"

To ensure a huge crowd, all workers in nearby textile plants could see the game at a reduced price if tickets were purchased at the various plants at which they worked. "Furniture Workers' Night" was an invitation for all furniture workers to see the game, also at a reduced price.

Although the Lexington and Thomasville teams were strong opponents, spectators respected the talents of players on both baseball teams, so never a curse word or derogatory comment was made by fans from either side.

Do You Remember These?

Above: When you and your family vacationed in a hot two-story beach house? *Courtesy of author.*

Right: When short bangs—the shorter the better—were in style? *Courtesy of author.*

Opposite, top: When cars had bumpers on the back and blinds in the rear window? *Courtesy of author.*

Opposite, bottom: When young girls had look-alike Shirley Temple ringlets? *Courtesy of author.*

PART II

Special Events

NEW JULIETTE LOW STAMPS AND GIRL SCOUTS

New Juliette Low stamps, issued in 1948 in honor of the founder of American Girl Scouts, arrived at Piedmont Triad post offices. They were placed on sale, and postmasters invited all Girl Scouts to be among the very first to purchase them. Belonging to a Girl Scout troop gave girls in the Piedmont Triad a chance to socialize with other young girls from different schools. Meetings were held weekly, usually in a church basement. Wearing their green uniforms—which included an across-the-shoulder sash to display the badges of which they were so proud—girls joined together to repeat the Girl Scout pledge and work on merit badges. The coveted Curved Bar was the ultimate reward for participating girls in this extremely popular program.

Spring and fall outings, each of which included one night of camping, became the highlight of the scouting year. Girls did not wear traditional uniforms on these casual trips. Shorts, T-shirts and sandals or tennis shoes replaced the formality of the Scout uniform. The campsite was usually a rustic one-room cabin at the edge of some generous farmer's property. An outdoor privy served as a toilet, and the only running water was an outside spigot. Cooking was done on an open fire built inside a circle of large rocks—juicy hot dogs roasted on long, skinny sticks. For dessert, Scouts enjoyed s'mores—roasted marshmallows and chunks of Hershey's milk chocolate bars sandwiched between two graham crackers.

Rustic Girl Scout cabin where Piedmont Triad scouts went twice a year for adventure, fun and merit badge work. *Courtesy of author.*

Rugged, lumpy cots lined two walls of the cabin. Curfew was called when the adult leaders extinguished the one overhead light bulb. The next morning, twenty to twenty-five worn-out but happy girls headed back home.

HALLOWEEN

Midway School, located "midway" between Lexington and Winston-Salem, sponsored a 1948 Halloween gala with ghosts, witches and jack-o'-lanterns for a filled-to-capacity audience. The festival began with a supper in the school cafeteria, sponsored by the teachers and parents. At 8:00

p.m., after the meal (delicious southern chicken pie and gravy), everyone moved into the gymnasium for the evening program presented by the students. Actors in the play *Witches and Ghosts* included Nancy Williard, Frances Head, Annetta Everhart, Willie Jo Harding, Sylvia Hedrick and Mack Shoaf.

Participants in a puppet show included Carolyn Calloway, Violet Berner, Kay Blakeley, Gene Crotts and Don Miller. Jewel Gobble sang "Halloween Night." Lorraine Beck was crowned queen of the festival. Other queen contestants included Betty Murphy, Elizabeth Cain and Clara Mae Ball. First place in the baby contest went to Patsy Clodfelter, second to Jimmy Berrier and third to Bonnie Sue Largen. The other babies in the contest were Richard Yokeley, Charles Hill, Ruth Lunsford, Danny Livengood, Bobby Jo Lawrence, Linda Graham, Junior Spry and Ramona Welch.

Davidson Hospital Women's Auxiliary also sponsored a Halloween party and dance. In the early hours of the evening, a children's party took place, with prizes being awarded for the best costumes. A grand march was held so that the costumes of the entrants could be seen properly. All attendees received favors and balloons. Then they enjoyed ice cream. After the children's party, adults enjoyed a dance. Jimmy Harris and his orchestra from High Point furnished the music.

Erlanger Mill Village in the Piedmont Triad always had a big Halloween fête. Sponsored by the Woman's Community Club, the annual event was held at Milton Hall, beginning at 6:00 p.m. Everyone knew to appear in costume. Games, contests and a cakewalk entertained those present. Homemade chicken stew and hot dogs provided a filling supper for all attendees.

Everybody loved Halloween. Southmont and Linwood schools began their celebrations with chicken pie suppers, served by the ladies of the Parent-Teacher Associations. Plates cost fifty cents. Following the meal, a motion picture feature was shown for a small admission. Added features included the cakewalk, fortunetelling, go-fishing, games, contests, carnival features and a turkey-calling contest. Ironically, the door prize for this kiddie event was a "piece of dress goods." I wonder how the young winner reacted to receiving a few yards of fabric.

Christmas Season

One of the highlights during the Christmas season was a contest sponsored by the *Dispatch*. The newspaper's coloring contest editor gave a one-dollar prize each day to the winner of the contest. The Christmas picture to be colored first appeared in the newspaper on December 6, 1954. A new picture followed for nine more days. The rules were specific:

- Contest is for boys and girls between the ages of 4 and 5.
- All entries must be postmarked within two days after publication.
- Prizes are awarded on basis of neatness and accuracy.
- The decision of the judges will be final.
- In case of a tie, duplicate prizes will be awarded.
- This contest will run for ten (10) days.

Annual Christmas parades took place in most Piedmont Triad cities and towns. With bright red and green lights streaming across various Main Streets and gold and silver banners draped around various poles and signs, high school bands played Christmas tunes and majorettes strutted from one end of town to the other. Beauty queens rode in convertibles; even if the weather was brutally cold, these lovely young ladies, dressed in strapless evening gowns, sat erect (but shivering) on the rear ledge of cars donated by local car dealerships. Families huddled together on each side of the street and watched in magical awe as decorated floats passed, and holiday elves tossed goodies to children standing nearby. Santa came last. Dressed in his red suit and black boots and holding a giant sack, he threw candy to those along the way.

The downtown stores and shops stayed open later on the evening of the Christmas parade. Storefront windows, sometimes decorated by professionals, glistened with the promise of what Santa might bring on Christmas Eve. Of course, toy displays proved to be the most popular, and each kid hoped that Santa was "making a list and checking it twice." A roving photographer snapped a picture of someone who became "Today's Lucky Shopper." A five-dollar prize was awarded after the person identified himself or herself to the local newspaper office.

In the '40s and '50s, families sent a lot of Christmas cards, even to the neighbors next door and across the street. Everyone proudly owned a holiday card holder and displayed, in their front rooms, pictures of Santa, elves, angels and the Virgin Mary with Joseph and baby Jesus.

Postmasters wrote articles for local Piedmont Triad newspapers to remind everyone of the importance of mailing early. Cards, letters and packages for delivery in distant states had to be mailed several days in advance of those intended for delivery in North Carolina and bordering states. All packages had to be packed in substantial cartons or wrappings and had to be well tied or sealed and correctly addressed, with street number, rural route and so on (no zip codes back then), as well as the return address of the sender. The following stipulations were issued:

> *Christmas greetings unsealed and bearing a 2-cent stamp cannot be returned to senders if they fail of delivery, but will be destroyed. Those sealed and bearing a 3-cent stamp and return address of sender will be returned to sender in case of non-delivery. Persons are asked to separate their mailings of Christmas greetings and tie them in packages marked "local" and "out of town," as the case may be. Any package may be sealed provided it bears an indication on the outside, either printed, written by hand, or typewritten stating that it may be opened for "postal inspection."*

Christmas Day was a time for seeing what Santa had left under the Christmas tree. A family meal, with turkey and all the side dishes, involved grandparents, parents, uncles, aunts and cousins.

An interesting after-Christmas moneysaving ritual in many Piedmont Triad homes pertained to ironing used Christmas gift paper, folding it neatly and storing it until the next year—when the family's presents would appear under the Christmas tree in the recycled gift wrap. Our red and green ribbon, which we also saved after ironing to a smooth and shiny perfection, was saved in the same box with the paper. We were already planning for the next Christmas gift-wrapping expedition a long twelve months away. Note that this was a long, long time before recycling became the norm. Our abundant cache of Christmas cards was sometimes used to make Christmas placemats. As well as I can remember, these were the

Opposite, top: Christmas morning came early—about 5:00 a.m.—for excited children who could not wait to see what Santa had left them. *Courtesy of author.*

Opposite, bottom: Little cowboys Randy and Wayne wear their new outfits to Grandmother's house on Christmas Day and pose for the entire family. *Courtesy of author.*

directions: roll out a foot (twelve inches) of Cut-Rite waxed paper. Cut. Roll out another foot of waxed paper. The next step is to use scissors to cut the front picture of each Christmas card (from the rest of the card) and place these single holiday scenes on one piece of the waxed paper. Cover with the second sheet of waxed paper. With a warm iron, press the two pieces of waxed paper together until they stick. Then decorate all four front-side edges with holiday tape of holly, snowflakes or berries. Use at next year's family Christmas dinner.

Occasionally, we were extremely disappointed after we had pulled a length of Cut-Rite from the box, torn the size we needed and discovered that the roll read, "Time to buy Cut-Rite."

Social, Civic and Study Events

In 1948, many social, civic and study events were held throughout the Piedmont Triad. A fall benefit bridge party was held by a Business and Professional Women's Club. The date was November 23, 1948, and an invitation issued to everyone indicated, "'Tis rumored that the prizes will be especially nice."

A call was issued for families to gather up their bundles of clothing for the Church World Service collection. The November 5, 1948 plea explained the need for garments: "Women overseas who have so little will not mind wearing those old dresses without the *new look*, so see what you can spare."

Members of the Civitan Club were entertained on the evening of October 27, 1948, by a group of young dancers that performed tap, ballet and acrobatic numbers in attractive dancing costumes. They were presented by the club's program chairman.

Daily newspapers in the Piedmont Triad reported on "society" events. Most of the time, these appeared anywhere from pages three to six. Descriptions were usually extremely detailed.

Tom Thumb Wedding

Invitations were announced as follows to an attractive Tom Thumb wedding:

Mr. and Mrs. John Wilton Walker
request the honor of your presence
at the marriage of their daughter
Mary Ann
To
Jimmie Leroy Raper
On Tuesday evening
May twenty-second
Cecil School Auditorium

The public and especially school patrons were urged to accept this invitation and witness the ceremony, which promised to be full of fun for everyone. A woman traveled throughout the Piedmont Triad assisting organizations in staging Tom Thumb weddings. She carried costumes with her and helped put on the program.

The Piedmont Triad Tom Thumb weddings originated with a real marriage on February 10, 1863, when little people Charles Sherwood Stratton and Lavinia Warren wed. The best man was George Washington Morrison ("Commodore") Nutt, a dwarf performer in P.T. Barnum's employ. The maid of honor was Minnie Warren, Lavinia's even smaller sister. The occasion became front-page news. Following their wedding, the couple was received by President Lincoln at the White House.

WSCS Meetings

The Woman's Society of Christian Service (WSCS) of Trinity Methodist Church met at the home of Mrs. Vallie Michael on Salisbury Street for the May 1959 meeting. Mrs. L.B. Koontz led the devotions, after which Mrs. T.G. Smith—assisted by Mrs. Elisha Allen, Mrs. W.C. Craven and Miss Polly Michael—gave an interesting program on "The Sanctity of the Christian Home." The business session followed, consisting of roll call, minutes, a treasurer report and reports from committees. A petition to be sent to Congress to abolish the manufacture and sale of liquor in North Carolina was passed and signed by all members.

The following research provides a unique and interesting twist to the long history of the WSCS:

> *MUSICIANS TO PLAY (1959)*
> *The Woman's Society will be represented on the program by its president, Mrs. Roy K. Smith.*
> *Music for the evening will be supplied by a teen-age musical group, the Velvet Tones. In the group are Luther Rabb, Pernell Alexander, Robert Green, Anthony Atherton, William Stull, Walter Jones and James [Jimi] Hendrix.*
> *Miss Ella Swift, one of the early-day "deaconesses," will be honored, along with past president of the Woman's Society.*

An interesting blog pertaining to that WSCS musical program explained one attendee's reactions: "Your expectations had been low when your Auntie made you don your reserved finest to attend a 1959 celebration sponsored by her Woman's Society of Christian Service. The only promise the event held in advance for you was that the *Seattle Sunday Times* reported there was to be a band—The Velvet Tones. You'd never heard of them."

WCTU Meetings

The various chapters of the Woman's Christian Temperance Union (WCTU) met in homes throughout the Piedmont Triad. Meetings were usually opened by reading the poem "Song of Peace":

> *This is my song. Oh God of all the nations,*
> *A song of peace for lands afar and mine.*
> *This is my home, the country where my heart is;*
> *Here are my hopes, my dreams, my sacred shrine.*
> *But other hearts in other lands are beating,*
> *With hopes and dreams as true and high as mine.*
>
> *My country's skies are bluer than the ocean,*
> *And sunlight beams on cloverleaf and pine.*
> *But other lands have sunlight too and clover,*
> *And skies are everywhere as blue as mine.*
> *Oh hear my song, oh God of all the nations,*
> *A song of peace for their land and for mine.*

Roll call followed. One of the programs presented at these meetings was a review of the movie *The Pay Off*, recently shown throughout various community high schools. The WCTU also sponsored a summer course at Mars Hill for young people, and members encouraged boys and girls to attend the session. After the business portion of the meeting, a speaker was introduced. At one such gathering, Mrs. Ida H. Conrad spoke on the life of Frances E. Willard, who at the age of nineteen was stricken with typhoid fever. She then decided to live for God; she was highly respected in the annals of history when she gave her life for the temperance cause.

Frances Willard's influence was instrumental in the passage of the Eighteenth (prohibition) and Nineteenth (women's suffrage) Amendments to the United States Constitution. She became the national president of the World's Woman's Christian Temperance Union in 1879 and remained president for nineteen years. She developed the slogan "Do everything" for the women of the WCTU in inciting lobbying, petitioning, preaching, publication and education. Her vision progressed to include federal aid for education, free school lunches, unions for workers, the eight-hour workday, work relief for the poor, municipal sanitation and boards of health, national transportation, strong anti-rape laws and protections against child abuse. At the conclusion of the program, members of the WCTU also heard a report of the Northwestern District meeting that was held in the First Baptist Church of Greensboro. The topic for that meeting had been "Organization and Cooperation."

Often, high school freshmen were special guests of this group. Having memorized a short temperance lesson from the organization's handbook, they recited the text from memory. The adults present voted on the best recitation, and a certificate was presented to the winner. Each of the young people present was required to sign a pledge promising that he or she would *never* drink alcohol.

VARIOUS CLUBS IN RURAL AREAS OF PIEDMONT TRIAD

Various clubs in the '40s and '50s provided an educational and entertaining few hours each week for those folks who wanted to get together in their own communities. Home Demonstration and 4-H Clubs sprang up in Welcome, Pilot, Bethesda, Reeds, Churchland, Fair Grove, Hasty, Silver Valley and other rural areas. The programs usually centered on sewing, canning,

Above: Members of 4-H canned fresh fruits and vegetables from their summer gardens in mason jars and stored them in cool basements and cellars. *Courtesy of Library of Congress.*

Left: This 4-H girl leads her calf for judging at a 4-H Club fair. *Courtesy of Library of Congress.*

gardening, flower arranging, cooking and animal husbandry. Club members always looked forward to various fairs, where they would exhibit their homemaking skills. Rather long records of these rural meetings appeared in local newspapers. The name of each club member was listed. The program topic and presenter were explored in minute detail. Business matters of the organization were revealed, and refreshments served received complete descriptions. Any guests were recognized in newsprint, and the next meeting date was announced.

POPULAR THEMED BANQUET

The seventh grade of the Piedmont Triad's Hasty School enjoyed a "Pan-American" banquet in May 1945. The classroom was decorated with pan-American flags and maps. Tables were vibrant with colored hats for the guests. Ralph Ontel Foster was master of ceremonies. A pan-American parade was given by students, who carried flags representing the twenty-one republics of the Pan-American Union. Joe Sink asked interesting questions on pan-America, and the master of ceremonies told jokes about various members of the seventh grade. Then the students were taken on a hike through the wheat fields of Buenos Aires and then taken to a tepee. There, Mr. West, principal, and Miss Maurie S. Pitt, supervisor, gave short talks. Six boys led the group in singing songs.

TAR HEEL GIRLS STATE

Special young women across the Piedmont Triad, as well as the entire state of North Carolina, were chosen each summer as delegates to the annual Tar Heel Girls State at Woman's College (now University of North Carolina–Greensboro). The weeklong conference gave these rising high school seniors an opportunity to learn "practical Americanism." They were chosen as delegates based on their qualities of leadership and scholarship. Members of the North Carolina American Legion Auxiliary supervised the selection of the attendees.

Mary Ann and Alice Lane at Girls State at the Woman's College in Greensboro the summer before entering their senior year at high school. *Courtesy of author.*

Those of us fortunate enough to attend Girls State in 1957 stayed in Woman's College dormitory rooms and wore dresses or skirts, blouses and our Sunday shoes every day, all day. We didn't need to have a curfew, and we knew not to make noise, date, smoke or drink. It was so different from the two-page memorandum that 2012 Girls State delegates received. Following are some of the stipulations for the 2012 "modern miss":

> *No denim, Capris, gauchos, blue jeans, or walking shorts. No tube tops, shoulder straps less than one inch, backless dresses, mid-drifts, shorts or skorts. No athletic shoes, flip flops, or beach sandals. No spaghetti straps. You may not date during the session. Alcoholic beverages, illegal drugs, or other contraband will not be brought on campus. No smoking. If you drive a car to Girls State, you must turn in your keys to the house mother after parking it in the designated parking area. A before and after inspection is made of each room. Citizens are responsible for any damages to her room or facilities.*

Note: The author of this book was elected lieutenant governor at the 1957 conference.

Big Annual Fair at Winston-Salem

Two of the entertainment features of the Winston-Salem and Forsyth County Fair of 1948 were "written up in a single issue of *Life* Magazine as the largest and most outstanding in their respective fields." According to Manager Tom S. Blum, "The same thing can be said of the entire Fair that opened Tuesday, October 5th, in North Carolina's Piedmont Triad's largest and most outstanding agricultural fair."

The two attractions that received such favorable notice in the nationally circulated magazine were the World of Mirth Shows, which provided the midway attractions at the Winston-Salem Fair, and the Chitwood's Auto Dare Devils, who entertained the crowds on Friday afternoon, October 8, and Saturday night, October 9, doing things with automobiles that had to be seen to be believed.

Joie Chitwood started his race car driving career in 1934. He was the first man ever to wear a safety belt at the Indy 500. Chitwood also operated the Joie Chitwood Thrill Show, an exhibition of auto stunt driving that became so successful that he gave up racing. Often called "Hell Drivers," he had five units that for more than forty years toured across North America, thrilling audiences in large and small towns alike with death-defying automobile stunts.

There was always plenty to interest all ages at the Winston-Salem Fair, and Mr. Blum declared that 1948 would be no exception. The famous George A. Hamid attractions were presented in front of the grandstand with an elaborate revue featuring music, dancing and pretty girls. Each evening concluded with thrilling fireworks.

George A. Hamid, born in 1896 in Broumana, Lebanon, learned tumbling on the dirt streets just as American boys learned baseball on the rural dirt diamonds. In 1907, he went to Marseilles, France, and joined Buffalo Bill's Wild West Show. The next year, when he arrived in the United States, he was taught to read and write in English by Annie Oakley and given his show business training by Buffalo Bill.

Wednesday, October 6 was "County School Day" at the Winston-Salem Fair, with all schoolchildren and teachers in Forsyth and adjoining counties admitted to the grounds free of charge as guests of the management. As an interesting aside, to comply with the law, those over twelve years of age had to pay the federal tax on free admissions.

DAVIDSON COUNTY AGRICULTURAL FAIR

Autumn days brought to mind the story rhyme, "The fair, the fair, the grand county fair with its noises and sideshows and fun everywhere." Women also got excited as they selected their best jars of quality canned foods for the exhibits. Mrs. C.A. Michael Jr. and Mrs. Marvin Hedrick of Southmont and Mrs. Alfred Craver of Hasty headed up this department. Mrs. Craver had worked on this section since the first year of the fair. She announced in a September 24, 1953 newspaper article, "The quality of the products gets better each year. Although there may not be as much canning due to freezing of foods, it is of much better quality. Canning is important; it is not replaced by freezing, for many foods can be canned that do not freeze well."

Homemakers were urged to carefully read the fair catalogue, select their best products and remember that all exhibits must be in standard-sized jars. Every jar must be neatly and plainly labeled, with the label on the front near the bottom of the jar. If two-piece lids were used, rings had to be left on to protect the top of the jar.

In judging jellies, jams, preserves, kraut and pickles, women were reminded that these jars would be opened in order for judges to taste the product and note texture and quality of the liquid. Then, every jar was always closed tightly so the product would keep throughout the week.

Lexington Chamber of Commerce president Charles Mauze announced plans for an Industrial Exhibit that would be an active, dramatic means of telling citizens the important story of industry and the American enterprise system. Mauze said, "People will come away from this year's exhibit with much more distinct and lasting impressions of the importance of industry." The chamber-sponsored exhibit featured many hundreds of dollars' worth of diversified manufactured goods, which were given away as attendance prizes.

An interesting and true aside regarding fair week concerns the housewives who refused to hang their laundry on the outside clotheslines because they were afraid that the "carnies" would steal their family's clothing.

The Saturday Morning Kiddie Show

The Saturday morning kiddie show admission price was nine cents. If kids didn't receive a weekly allowance, they were traditionally given a dime by their parents. After paying to get inside the theater, there was also a decision of what to buy at the concession stand with that extra penny. Popcorn and drinks costs ten to twenty-five cents each. A Hershey's, Fifth Avenue or Snickers bar each cost another dime. A Tootsie Pop was about the only penny-priced goodie. Before the cartoons opened the movie program, kids were invited onstage for a talent show. Wearing frilly costumes and black tap shoes, girls from various schools of dance performed. Boys played their trumpets, banjos and ukuleles. A cherished prize—a free pass to the next kiddie show—was awarded to the winner of the talent show.

On December 5, 1945, Lexington's Carolina Theatre and several surrounding apartments and stores were destroyed by fire. When the town's fire horn blew and citizens counted the toots, they realized that the fire was on Lexington's South Main Street. Rushing to the scene, grown-ups and children alike sat silently across the street on the grassy knoll between the post office and First Methodist Church. Some old-timers still remember the name of the movie that had played that night—*Home in Indiana*, starring Walter Brennan, Jeanne Crain and Charlotte Greenwood.

Some folks recalled that the loss was estimated at over $350,000, and firefighters used so much of the city's water that the pressure dropped dramatically in the system. Others reported that at war's end, the city sought to make long-needed improvements in the fire department's equipment inventory, purchasing hoses, nozzles, ladders and other equipment they could not buy during the war. The city also purchased an American LaFrance model-800 pumper in 1948 and a second one in 1952. Finally, in 1959, the department received its first aerial apparatus—an American LaFrance eighty-five-foot ladder truck.

The day after the Carolina Theatre fire, officials of North Carolina Theatres Inc. of Charlotte arrived in Lexington to confer with Mrs. Alma H. Crowell, representing the J.T. Hedrick estate, with respect to possible plans for restoring the theater. T. Norman Owen, fire chief and building inspector, was quoted in a newspaper article as stating, "Sherwood Brockwell, for many years state fire marshal, is expected to arrive here today or tomorrow from Raleigh to cooperate in making a thorough inspection of the walls of the burned out building with a view to determining what portion of the walls should be razed and what might be salvaged and left standing for reconstruction."

Immediately, there were talks of building a new movie theater, the Center. Another option was expanding and renovating the existing 250-seat Granada Theatre on North Main Street. A decision was made to rebuild the Carolina to the tune of about $25,000. The first movie show in the new building was *The Paleface*, a 1948 Technicolor comedy western directed by Norman Z. McLeod, starring Bob Hope as "Painless" Potter and Jane Russell as Calamity Jane. In the film, Hope sang the song "Buttons and Bows" (by Jay Livingston and Ray Evans), which became his greatest hit by far when it came to record sales. The song also won the Academy Award for Best Song that year.

The plot concerned Peter "Painless" Potter, a dentist of doubtful competence. Out west, after the partner of Calamity Jane is killed while trying to discover who's been illegally selling guns to Indians, the cowardly Painless ends up married to Jane, who needs to keep her true identity a secret. One day, while protecting everyone during a holdup, Jane gives all the credit to Painless, who becomes the townsfolk's "brave" new hero.

DRIVE-IN THEATER

Warm spring and summer nights found teens at a regional drive-in theater. This was the perfect place to enjoy a movie, hot dogs and some Cokes from the concession stand—and maybe even a little "necking." Since each person in a car had to pay his or her price of admission, it was not unheard of for young folks to duck in the floorboard of the car so they could dodge admission charges.

The drive-in concession stand sold mouthwatering hot dogs, hamburgers and French fries. Ice-cold Cokes hit the spot on hot summer nights. A playground with sliding board and swings was located between the front row of cars and the outdoor screen. Occasionally, someone would inadvertently honk his or her car horn, and practically every other car would respond with a warning honk. If the movie reel broke—which it was prone to do—the sound of fifty car horns alerted the management of the problem, and it was soon fixed. Another occurrence involved driving off with the speakers after the movie had concluded—unintentional, of course.

Roman Togas and Buying Slaves

The mid-1950s brought some unusual events. None was as strange as our Latin Club initiation. "Latin?" you may ask. Yes, all college-bound freshmen and sophomores were required to take two years of high school Latin. Nothing wrong with that, you might say. True, but being a Latin scholar also meant mandatory attendance at Latin Club functions, the highlight (or lowlight) of which was an annual "Buying of Slaves" ceremony. Most of us at that time were too young or too innocent to realize that slavery in any form was wrong, but we knew that if we wanted a decent grade in the course, we'd have to toe the line, which we all did.

The ceremony usually took place one autumn evening in the backyard of a fellow student who desperately needed extra brownie points. Everyone in the club—that meant everyone who was taking Latin, and that meant the majority of freshmen and sophomores—was required to dress in traditional Roman garb. Usually that consisted of white bedsheets draped around our

Roman togas were donned by members of the Latin Club during their acceptance into that popular high school organization. *Courtesy of westcoastconnection.com.*

bodies and over one shoulder. Some togas were belted with flannel bathrobe belts, and some were not. Garlands of artificial greenery crowned our heads. We wore sandals.

Our Latin teacher, Miss Jones, orchestrated the ritual. Sophomores bid on their desired slaves. The quarter or fifty cents went into the Latin Club treasury. Potential slaves, the freshmen, stood on an overturned tin washtub while the Roman soldiers and gentry bid. Highest bidders owned a slave for an entire school day. The most popular girls and boys were chosen, not for their "servitude abilities" but because of their pretty or handsome looks. After all, who wouldn't want his or her slave to be good looking and popular? All freshmen in the Latin Club were offered on the "slavery block," and all were sold; some brought more money than others. All money went toward an October day trip to the state fair in Raleigh.

Slave Day occurred soon after the auction. For one entire school day, slaves were required to follow their owner's bidding. They toted books, carried cafeteria trays and escorted owners to various classes. They sang "Quo, O Quo" ("Where, Oh Where, Has My Little Dog Gone?") as they marched up and down the hallways of the high school. They substituted for their owners in games of "verb baseball." When 3:15 p.m. came, they were freed, and freshmen looked forward to the next fall, when they would be the ones buying.

Later in the fall, a few select Latin Club students were coerced into volunteering one entire Sunday to ride with their Latin teacher to the Crossnore Orphanage, located deep in the mountains of North Carolina. Our mission was to deliver to the orphans a trunk load of used (but clean and usable) clothes and shoes that we had collected through our Latin Club clothing drive. Those students who volunteered to go received bonus points on their end-of-semester grade.

We were on our way. My best friend Sarah climbed into the front seat of Miss Jones's car. The remaining three of us chose the back seat. Remember, this was a Sunday morning. Miss Jones was dressed as if she were going to church. She even wore a fancy hat. We were barely out of her driveway and on our two-hour drive to Crossnore Orphanage, nestled on the side of a mountain at a crossroads in the middle of nowhere, when Miss Jones removed her hat, handed it to Sarah and said, "Wear this while I drive." Sarah didn't know what to do or say, so she carefully and tenderly held Miss Jones's hat on her lap. "No, wear it," Miss Jones insisted. By this time, the three of us in the back seat were trying our best to stifle our giggles. We knew that we'd be in big trouble if we were heard laughing. Sarah wore

Miss Jones's hat all the way to the orphanage, at which time she removed it and placed it on Miss Jones's head. We delivered the boxes of clothing to a supervisor, got back in the car and headed home. Sarah scrambled for a place in the back seat for the return trip. Heading back home, Miss Jones—who wore her hat all the way—suggested that we sing Latin songs. We started with "Old McDonald."

"We'll do 'cow' first," she instructed. She would lead. Everybody would follow. And then duck, sheep, pig, horse, dog and, last of all, cat. Everybody got that? Ready, set, begin! And we all sang with gusto and glee:

> *Galus est Agricola. E-I-E-I-O*
> *In agris elus equi sung. E-I-E-I-O*
> *Hic Hinniunt. Ibi hinniunt.*
> *Hi-b—hinniunt oblique!*

Our singing was loud and clear. Old McDonald himself would have been very, very pleased.

Do You Remember These?

Previous, top: When extreme modesty was almost sacred? *Courtesy of author.*

Previous, bottom: When girls wore socks with sandals? *Courtesy of author.*

Right: When men proudly owned brand-new automobiles and parked them at the street curb with the keys in the ignition? *Courtesy of author.*

Below: When "sack" dresses—going back to the 1920s style—were popular? *Courtesy of author.*

PART III

Moments to Remember

Junior–Senior Banquet and Prom

The big spring event for the Piedmont Triad was the Junior-Senior Banquet and Prom, held at the country club on May 18, 1945, one year. The banquet featured food prepared by the mothers of juniors. A typical meal was baked ham, a mound of mashed potatoes with green garden peas scooped on top, beets (for that red color), cooked carrots (for that orange color), homemade yeast rolls, real butter and sweetened iced tea. For dessert, homemade cake with ice cream finished off the meal. About thirty freshman and sophomore girls, selected by their teachers, donned white dresses with ruffled pink pinafore aprons and served the meal.

At the 1945 banquet, the president of the junior class served as toastmaster, and the president of the senior class spoke to the group. Members of the faculty, the chairman of the school board, the superintendent, Mrs. L.E. Andrews and the class mascots were special guests for the occasion.

In charge of the decorations, Mrs. L.A. Martin chose a Mexican theme, which was carried out throughout the country club. Parents of the members of the senior class assisted Mrs. Banks Peeler, the chairwoman. A group of underclassmen distributed gifts to each of the seniors. After the banquet was over, the tables were removed and dancing was enjoyed.

On prom night, the usual eleven o'clock curfew was extended until midnight.

Parties Honor Brides-to-Be, but Rules Apply

Parties for Piedmont Triad brides-to-be were elaborate in the 1940s and 1950s. Most of these festivities were held in the homes of friends or relatives. It was not unusual to have seven or eight tables of bridge in formal living rooms decorated with white chrysanthemums and red roses. The bride's place was marked with a miniature wedding cake. Winners in the bridge game earned prizes—a luncheon set or a hand-painted salad bowl. Guests showered the bride with miscellaneous gifts, and the hostess was expected to present her with a place setting in her "best" china pattern. In addition, special out-of-town guests received gifts from the hostess.

Bridal parties in the '50s were extremely popular. Many hostesses entertained the bride-to-be, her mother and sisters and the groom's mother and sisters with afternoon bridge parties. *Courtesy of author.*

Gifts for the bride and groom often consisted of fine silver trays, bonbon dishes and various pieces of the bride's chosen silver pattern. *Courtesy of author.*

When the bridal shower details appeared in the local newspaper, married guests were always listed as Mrs. So-and-so and not with their given first names. One important "no-no" surfaced: none of the bride's or groom's relatives could host a shower at which gifts were expected. That was considered to be in the *worst* taste in the South. In fact, the exact word was "tacky."

Minstrel Shows: Realistic or Deceiving?

Amateur performances of minstrel shows continued until the late 1950s in high schools and local theaters. The typical minstrel performance had three acts. The troupe first danced onto stage, exchanged wisecracks and sang songs. The second part featured a variety of entertainments, including pun-filled stump speeches. The final act consisted of a slapstick musical plantation skit or a sendup of a popular play. Minstrel songs and sketches featured several stock characters, most popularly the slave and the dandy. These were further divided into archetypes such as the mammy; her counterpart, the old darky; the provocative mulatto wench; and the black soldier. Minstrels claimed that their songs and dances were authentically black, although today the extent of the black influence remains debated.

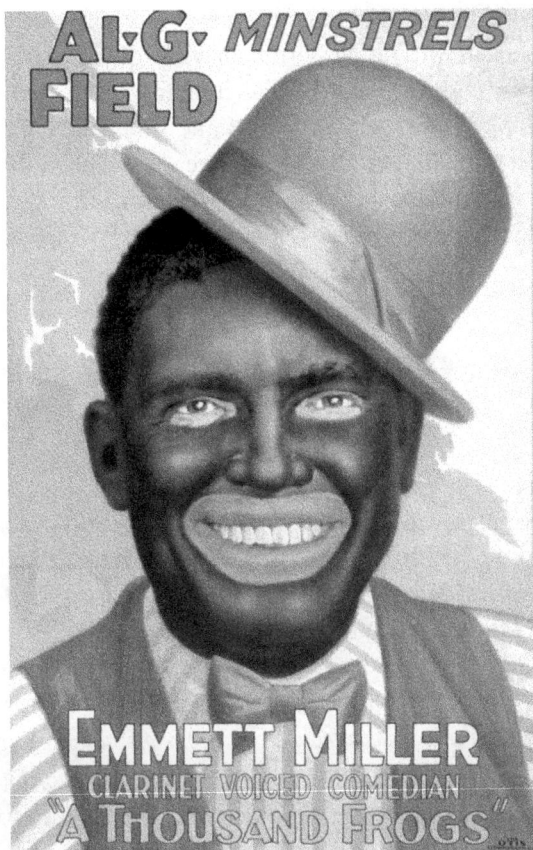

Minstrel shows were extremely popular in the '50s, although some citizens believed that they were controversial. *Courtesy of Library of Congress.*

As African Americans began to score legal and social victories against racism and assert political power, minstrelsy lost popularity. Blackface minstrelsy had been the first distinctly American theatrical form. In the 1820s and 1840s, it was at the core of the rise of an American music industry, and for several decades, it provided the lens through which white America saw black America. On the one hand, it had strongly racist aspects; on the other, it afforded white Americans a singular and broad awareness of what some whites considered significant aspects of black American culture to be.

Although the minstrel shows were extremely popular, being "consistently packed with families from all walks of life and every ethnic group," they were also controversial. Racial integrationists decried them as falsely showing happy slaves while at the same time making fun of them. Segregationists thought that such shows were "disrespectful" of social norms, portrayed runaway slaves with sympathy and would undermine the southerners' "peculiar institution." The popularity of minstrel shows declined greatly.

"WHAT IT WAS, WAS [ANDY GRIFFITH'S] FOOTBALL"

The date was May 1952, and at the High Point Rotary Club's annual Ladies' Night social, the guest performers were at that time relatively unknown: Andy Griffith and his first wife, Barbara. The couple was paid fifty dollars to provide the evening's entertainment. Andy told stories and also gave his rendition of "What It Was, Was Football":

It was back last October, I believe it was.
We was going to hold a tent service off at this college town,
And we got there about dinner time on Saturday.
Different ones of us thought that we ought to get us a mouthful to eat before
we set up the tent.
So we got off the truck and followed this little bunch of people
Through this small little bitty patch of woods there,
And we came up on a big sign that says, "Get something to Eat Here."

I went up and got me two hot dogs and a big orange drink,
And before I could take a mouthful of that food,
This whole raft of people come up around me and got me to where I couldn't
eat nothing, up like,

Well, we commenced to go through all kinds of doors and gates and I don't
know what-all,
And I looked up over one of 'em and it says, "North Gate."

Moments to Remember

We kept on a-going through there, and pretty soon we come up on a young boy
  and he says,
"Ticket, please."
And I says, "Friend, I don't have a ticket.
I don't even know where it is that I'm a-going!"
Well, he says, "Come on out as quick as you can."
And I says, "I'll do 'er; I'll turn right around the first chance I get."

Well, we kept on a-moving through there,
And pretty soon everybody got where it was that they was a-going,
Because they parted and I could see pretty good
And what I seen was this whole raft of people a-sittin on these two banks
And a-lookin at one another across this pretty little green cow pasture.

Somebody had took and drawed white lines all over it and drove posts in it,
And I don't know what all,
And I looked down there and I seen five or six convicts a running up and down
And a-blowing whistles.
And then I looked down there and I seen these pretty girls wearin' these little
  bitty short dresses
And a-dancing around, and so I thought I'd sit down and see what it was that
  was a-going to happen.

About the time I got set down good I looked down there
And I seen thirty or forty men come a-runnin' out of one end of a great big
  outhouse down there
And everybody where I was a-settin got up and hollered!
And I asked this fella that was a sittin' beside of me,
"Friend, what is it that they're a-hollerin' for?"
Well he whopped me on the back and he says,
"Buddy, have a drink." I says,
"Well, I believe I will have another big orange."
It got it and set back down.

When I got there again I seen that the men had got in two little bitty bunches
  down there
Real close together, and they voted.
They elected one man apiece,
And them two men come out in the middle of that cow pasture

And shook hands like they hadn't seen one another in a long time.
Then a convict came over to where they was a-standin',
And he took out a quarter and they commenced to odd man right there!
After a while I seen what it was they was odd-manning for.
It was that both bunchesful of them wanted this funny lookin little
  pumpkin to play with.
And I know, friends, that they couldn't eat it because they kicked it the
  whole evenin'
And it never busted.

Both bunchesful wanted that thing.
One bunch got it and it made the other bunch just as mad as they could be!
Friends, I seen that evenin' the awfulest fight that I ever have seen in all
  my life!
They would run at one-another and kick one-another
And throw one another down and stomp on one another
And grind their feet in one another
And I don't know what—
All and just as fast as one of 'em would get hurt,
They'd take him off and run another one on!

Well, they done that as long as I set there, but pretty soon this boy that
  had said
"Ticket please," He come up to me and said,
"Friend, you're gonna have to leave because it is that you don't have a ticket."
And I says, "Well, all right." And I got up and left.

I don't know friends, to this day, what it was that they was a doin' down there,
But I have studied about it.
I think it was that it's some kindly of a contest where they see which
  bunchful of them men can take that pumpkin and run from one end of
  that cow pasture to the other'n without either getting knocked down—
  'er steppin' in somethin'.

After Andy's wonderful rendition, Barbara danced. Then Andy and
Barbara, with backup from various Rotarians and their spouses, sang a
variety of songs. The Griffiths' personalities shone, and as the old Piedmont
Triad saying goes, "A good time was had by all."

Eight years later, on October 3, 1960, *The Andy Griffith Show* first aired, televised by CBS. Andy Griffith portrayed a widowed sheriff in the fictional small community of Mayberry, North Carolina. His life was complicated by an inept but well-meaning deputy, Barney Fife (Don Knotts); a spinster aunt and housekeeper, Aunt Bee (Frances Bavier); and a young son, Opie (Ron Howard). Local ne'er-do-wells, bumbling pals and temperamental girlfriends further complicated the plot.

The series was a major hit, never placing lower than seventh in the Nielsen ratings and ending its final season at number one. It has been ranked by *TV Guide* as the ninth-best show in television history.

FUN AND GAMES: FROM INNOCENT HOPSCOTCH TO THE DDT TRUCK

Regular hopscotch is a children's game that was played in the Piedmont Triad, either with several players or alone. The players tossed a small object into the numbered spaces of a pattern of rectangles outlined on the ground. Then they would hop or jump through the spaces to retrieve the object.

Children could lay the hopscotch course on the ground, either scratched out in dirt or drawn with chalk on pavement. Designs varied, but the course was usually composed of a series of linear squares interspersed with blocks of two lateral squares. Traditionally, the course ended with a "safe" or "home" base in which the player could turn before completing the reverse trip. The home base was a square, a rectangle or a semicircle. The squares were numbered in the sequence in which they were to be hopped.

The first player tossed the marker (typically a stone, coin or bean bag) into the first square. The marker had to land completely within the designated square without touching a line or bouncing out. The player then hopped through the course, skipping the square with the marker in it. Single squares had to be hopped on one foot. For the first single square, either foot could be used. Side-by-side squares were straddled, with the left foot landing in the left square and the right foot landing in the right square. Optional squares were marked "safe," "home" or "rest" and were considered neutral squares and could be hopped through in any manner without penalty. After hopping into the "safe," "home" or "rest," the player had to then turn around and return through the course on one or two legs depending on the square until she reached the square with her marker. Then she had to retrieve her marker and continue the course as stated without touching a line or stepping into a square with another player's marker.

Upon successfully completing the sequence, the player continued the turn by tossing the marker into square number two and repeating the pattern.

If while hopping through the court in either direction the player stepped on a line, missed a square or lost balance, the turn ended. Players began their turns where they last left off. The first player to complete one course for every numbered square on the court won the game. (It's amazing how quickly we kids mastered the game with its rather complicated rules but struggled mightily with the "ninth" multiplication table.)

Piedmont Triad boys played marbles on circles drawn in the dirt. Girls found various ways to entertain themselves. Jump rope was a favorite. They chanted as they jumped: "Cinderella dressed in yellow went upstairs to kiss her fella. How many kisses did she give him?" In addition, girls enjoyed games like kick the can, ring-a-lee-bo and hide the flag. Then, after a big downpour, there were always those wonderful mud puddles in which to splash. If someone was really lucky, he or she could retrieve a penny from a muddy gutter. Once in a while, boys would chase the girls with strings of wild onions, swishing their legs with the stinky plants. Kids used their imaginations. Especially familiar was our act of sticking baseball cards into the spokes of a bike to transform it into a motorcycle. We were innovative and creative; we played hard and fast. We had never heard of play dates.

During late summer evenings, kids had different play activities. Catching lightning bugs and putting them in jars became a favorite pastime. Picking blackberries and getting chigger bites was not the fun it was reported to be. We made forts in the woods before dark; roller-skated with heavy, clunky skates (which required a key to tighten shoes to skates); climbed trees; looked for four-leaf clovers; and got home after curfew time, which resulted in getting your legs switched with yellow bell bush branches with the leaves stripped. But the punishment was usually worth the pain and embarrassment when kids were late getting home, especially if they had lost all sense of time because they had been dancing down the street, following the truck that sprayed clouds of stinky DDT in their faces and singing the chant:

Moments to Remember

Ain't no bears out tonight.
Grandpa killed them all last night.

Hot summer days usually found teenagers in the Piedmont Triad flocking to various public pools in their neighborhoods. The admission ticket cost only fifty cents for an entire afternoon of swimming and diving. Wire baskets were available for their shorts, halters and shoes. Many "double dog dares" brought backflips from the diving board. When guys tired of the water and of showing off their skills, dunking the teen girls in the pool, many of them retreated to the upstairs open-air pavilion to purchase miniature bags of Lay's potato chips and Big Oranges or Dr. Peppers. It wasn't long before the girls followed. Everyone listened to jukebox records and either participated in the popular dances to the tune of "Sixty Minute Man" or "Ruby, Ruby" or became interested bystanders. There were always old friends, and new, to meet. Changing from their bathing suits to stylish peg leg pants, guys looked groovy. Girls wore bobby socks rolled down to their ankles and even cut off the tops of old socks and put them under the folds to make them nice and thick. Girls often pulled their hair back in buns and wrapped artificial flowers around the knots. They wore jeans rolled up, with scarves around their waists and also around their necks. Although this fashion proved to be extremely warm in the summer, girls still wanted to look stylish, even in the heat.

When things got dull, something new usually appeared. The "Picture Man" came to various neighborhoods, and for a quarter, cowboys and cowgirls could have their pictures made on his pony. During the hottest days, kids listened and looked for the ice cream truck to come into their neighborhood. They could usually hear his truck bell ringing long before he arrived. They had time to run back home and plead for money to buy a popsicle, ice cream sandwich or snow cone.

RICHARD G. WALSER, A FAVORITE PIEDMONT TRIAD AUTHOR, HONORED

Richard G. Walser, professor and author, was honored at an April 1948 autograph tea at the Davidson County Public library under the joint sponsorship of the bookstore and the Sorosis Study Club. The public was invited to attend. The bookstore had already secured Mr. Walser's latest book, *North Carolina in the Short Story*, published by the University of North Carolina Press. This publication received wide acclaim and complimentary reviews.

Mr. Walser received his AB and MA degrees from the University of North Carolina. He taught at Linwood after graduating from college and was a member of the Lexington High School faculty for several years. He also taught for a while at the University of North Carolina–Chapel Hill and North Carolina State College.

BETTY CROCKER HOMEMAKER OF TOMORROW AWARD

In September 1953, General Mills announced a new program that would launch in January 1955 called the Betty Crocker Search for the American Homemaker of Tomorrow, which was aimed at domesticating high school girls. The program was meant "to focus national attention on the so-called 'forgotten career' of homemaking, and on the untiring job being done by America's high schools to develop citizens and homemakers of the future." The written exam tested girls on their family relationships, spiritual and moral values, child development and care, health and safety, utilization and conservation, money management, recreation and use of leisure time, home care and beautification, community participation and continuing education.

Winners were selected based on test scores and "personal qualities" from observations and interviews. The national winner received a $5,000 scholarship, the opportunity to take an educational three-month tour of the United States and a specially designed golden pin, which many women still possess and cherish today.

The program continued to grow each year by number of participants and awarded scholarship money. In 1973, the program was opened up to males. The committee revised some rules, and the name of the program was changed to the Betty Crocker Search for Leadership in Family Living. The name was changed once again in 1977 to the General Mills Search for Leadership in Family Living. After the program's twenty-two-year reign, it came to an end.

Moments to Remember

Note: The author of this book cherishes the gold pin she received as the 1955 winner from Lexington Senior High School and still enjoys reading the various blogs from other winners throughout the Piedmont Triad.

BETTY JO RING, MISS NORTH CAROLINA 1954

It is probably safe to say that practically everyone over the age of twelve who was living in the Piedmont Triad in June 1954 knew the name Betty Jo Ring. This pretty and popular English teacher at Lexington Senior High School won the crown of Miss North Carolina. When asked how she felt about winning the pageant, she responded, "Gracious, all the adjectives that mean terrific cannot do my feelings justice—they just sound insincere." In a newspaper interview, Miss Ring offered praise of the pageant and also urged other young ladies to consider entering future contests to see if they, too, could win the honor.

Miss Ring spoke sincerely about what might be a parental objection to having daughters interested in the pageant. She elaborated by saying, "This is not a Miss Apple Core Contest, and it is nothing to be frowned upon. My strongest supporters have been my church organizations, the Woman's Christian Temperance Union, the PTA, the Lexington school board, the Classroom Teachers' Association, the North Carolina Foundation Association, and my mother and dad." She outlined the following reasons for praising the pageant:

The motto, Modesty first, Ambition and Success are challenges. To know that you even have been considered makes one feel she has an obligation to herself and to others who know of her new undertaking. Participation in a local pageant—no matter how large or small it may be—may give a girl butterflies for awhile, but it also gives her worlds of poise that she may not be conscious of gaining. Winning or losing in a local pageant teaches the mature girl to be a good sport. On becoming a local winner the new "Miss Wonderful Town" is invited to participate in numerous civic functions. If she is any woman of backbone, she will learn that "you do, when you have to." But more important, she will see that no matter how distasteful that task may be to her personally (and there are no functions unbecoming to the motto) that she is not the one giving but she

61

is gaining. Her views will broaden and no matter how dense she thinks she is, association with civic leaders and the learned town fathers is sure to rub something beneficial off on her.

As Miss North Carolina, Betty Jo Ring understood the importance of young ladies' preparation for pageant appearances. She believed that participation included making a girl more aware of her assets and liabilities…and making her do something about them. Also, the participant would come to realize that she is not the only one involved because her family, friends, members of her sponsoring club and all she comes in contact with are human beings; therefore, she would acquire a great deal of tact in getting along with everyone. She would become more adaptable and learn to take constructive criticism.

Interestingly, in 1954, Miss Ring spoke of what made a "true lady":

She never stoops to gossip of destructive criticism. She learns when to talk and when to refrain from playing "motor mouth." She will learn to think—to brush up on world affairs—social and political, and to discuss them intelligently. A true lady will also learn that the expert judges will look at a girl's eyes as well as her legs. Newspaper men, photographers, and autograph seekers are doing her a favor. She will reciprocate with cooperation, toleration, patience, and quick but kind humor.

The new Miss North Carolina warned would-be contestants: "Now don't shake your head. All these benefits are not superhuman and can come to every girl. I have never seen any woman who does not possess some amount of everything mentioned. The lucky women are those who have a chance to participate in a Jaycee pageant." Miss Ring stressed the human nature quality associated with participation in the pageant: "Truly, the most important item to learn is that each girl will make mistakes, but if she has any maturity, these will be her greatest teacher."

ACTUALLY LIVING THE HISTORICAL MOMENT OF INTEGRATION

In the fall of 1958, Greensboro's Woman's College admitted five black students. These young women were assigned to rooms on a first-floor hall of the Anna Howard Shaw Dormitory, just inside the side entrance to the dorm. Their names were Jewell Anthony, Patricia Jones, Clara Withers, Lily Wiley and Edith Mayfield. No white girls were assigned to this hall. Memories of this occasion remain vivid in the mind of the author of this book. I was there, on the second floor in the same dorm, as a freshman at the college.

Although I don't remember the integration being especially traumatic or uncomfortable, I'm sure my African American dorm mates definitely had to make adjustments; they had come from all-black high schools, just as the rest of us had graduated from all-white institutions. I think the "arrival at school" incident that literally broke the ice occurred late that first afternoon after most of us had checked into our rooms and were sitting on the side steps of the dorm waiting for the cafeteria to open.

A taxi pulled up and stopped in front of us. "Is this Shaw Dorm?" the driver asked. We told him it was. He got out of the cab, as did his passenger, who had obviously flown into Greensboro and taken this taxi to the college. The driver opened the truck and delivered several large suitcases to the pavement. Then, the next incident took us by surprise. This young white girl saw five African American girls sitting on the steps, stared directly at all five, snapped her fingers, pointed to her luggage, paid the cab driver and waited (not so patiently) for her luggage to be carried into Shaw.

I think one of us nervously spoke up, not really knowing what to do or say. I remember it went something like this: "We're all your new dorm mates, so we'll all help you carry your things inside." With that, we each grabbed a suitcase or box and headed inside.

For me and my roommate, Sylvia Leonard, this unique welcoming turned out to be the beginning of a congenial association with our five new neighbors in Shaw.

In a 1991 oral history interview with Edith Mayfield Wiggins, she recalled her experiences:

> *I went there in the fall of 1958 and it was still the Woman's College of the University of North Carolina. I had graduated in the spring from William Penn High School, which is an all-black high school in High Point, North Carolina. I lived in Shaw my freshman year. Shaw Residence Hall was an all-freshman dorm. As a matter of fact, Shaw was at the head of what was called the "quad." What was unique about my living arrangements, I was one of five black women that had*

Sylvia Leonard (front row, center), my roommate at Woman's College in Greensboro in the fall of 1958, when Shaw Dormitory was first integrated. *Courtesy of author.*

been admitted that year. Two of us had rooms—there were two sets of roommates, and then there was an extra person, so that meant there were three rooms, but no other white students were put on that end of the hall with us. So we had a whole wing of Shaw Dormitory to ourselves because we were black. The other rooms were completely empty that entire year. As a matter of fact, some of the white students were sleeping three to a room.

Let me talk about a group of women that provided a good deal of support. And those were the maids, Annie and Victoria. Annie Reeves was the first-floor maid in Shaw, and Victoria Johnson was the second- and third-floor maid in Shaw. And I tell you, I loved those women. They were my mothers, they were my surrogate mothers. We did more crying on their shoulders about everything. We were with them every day. On weekends they would pick us up and take us—Annie in particular—would take us to her house and to church.

How they made the black students look just like the white students in our yearbook picture? I always have to look for myself on that page. Can you believe that. It's very—I mean it says—it's as lightened as it could be, right. Here's Clara. Clara was really dark. You have to really look to find her on that picture.

Sylvia still remembered Lily saying to her, "Your knees really have personality when you wear Bermuda shorts!"

A year and a half later, four A&T college students, now known as the "Greensboro Four," went into the downtown Woolworth's and sat at the all-white lunch counter.

THE MAY DAY MAYPOLE DANCE: PURE OR SINISTER?

"If winter comes, can spring be far behind?" could well have been the motto of the Student Government Association at High Point College. That organization sponsored the election of the campus May Queen. Chosen from the senior class by the members of the student body to reign at the May Day dance was Jane Martin of Denton. She had been recently added to *Who's Who in American Colleges and Universities.*

The Queen of May, or May Queen, is a name that has two distinct but related meanings—as a mythical figure and as a holiday personification. In 1958, the May Queen was a girl who rode and walked at the front of a parade for May Day celebrations. She usually wore a white gown to symbolize purity and a tiara or crown. Her duty was to begin the May Day celebrations. She was crowned by flowers and made a speech before certain age groups, who danced around a Maypole celebrating youth and spring time. The dance involved an intricate weaving of colorful ribbons, in a much-practiced ritual, around the pole.

The history behind the May Queen was not always positive. According to folklore, the tradition once had a sinister twist: the May Queen was put to death once the festivities were over. The veracity of this belief is difficult to establish, but while in truth it might just be an example of an anti-ritual, the occult and human sacrifice are still to be found in popular culture today. *The Wicker Man*, a cult horror film starring Christopher Lee, is a prominent example of these associations.

In the Piedmont Triad, the celebration of May Day was extremely popular in the 1940s and 1950s. One esteemed and prolific photographer shot movies of the May Day celebration on land bordering the city pool.

SUMMER CAMP, CHIGGERS AND MOSQUITOES

Many times, Piedmont Triad boys' and girls' sole summer vacation was a week at "Church Camp." Johns River Valley Camp, in the North Carolina mountains, brought young people together for a week of Bible study, hiking, swimming in the river and morning calisthenics before

Right: The bell at the old well house at Johns River Valley Camp in the mountains of North Carolina. This was the designated "meeting place." *Courtesy of author.*

Previous page: Girls at Johns River Valley Camp are ready for their swim in the lake. *Courtesy of author.*

breakfast in front of the mess hall. Four elderly women, who lived in a small cottage on the campgrounds, prepared three hearty meals each day. Campers served themselves family style at long tables. Bible study filled the morning hours. After lunch, there was that mandatory "rest period" in hot cabins that smelled of mildew. Boys stayed on one side of the grounds and girls on the other. "Never the two would meet on each other's designated turf."

There was a large centrally located bathhouse with toilets, lavatories and showers for each gender. When campers arrived on Sunday afternoon, the nurses gave them a dose of milk of magnesia—whether they needed it or not—to ensure necessary elimination. Afternoons included long hikes. This was about the only time the boys and girls were allowed to walk together, introduce themselves and chat. When the camp counselor blew his or her whistle, everyone changed walking partners.

Campers meet outside the dining hall in preparation for the afternoon's hiking activities. *Courtesy of author.*

After supper, campers met at the "big bell" and marched single file up a steep incline to "Vesper Hill." Songs, devotions and prayers completed each day at camp. "Lights out," in each cabin, occurred at nine o'clock sharp. By the end of camp week, everyone had made new friends, renewed their faith and made various and sundry lariats to take home.

Opposite: In a historic event, classmates met at the author's home to watch the inauguration of Ike on the family's black-and-white television set. *Courtesy of author.*

IKE'S INAUGURATION, 1953

The first inauguration of Dwight D. Eisenhower as the thirty-fourth president of the United States was held on January 20, 1953. Chief Justice Fred M. Vinson administered the oath of office to Eisenhower. Richard Nixon was sworn in as vice president by Senator William Knowland of California.

Because elementary schools did not have A/V rooms or even television sets, some teachers made arrangements for children in their classes to watch the swearing in on television sets in private homes within walking distance of the school. Small groups of students, on their best behavior, viewed the historic event, thanked the hostess and walked back to school. The classroom discussion that followed proved to be a firsthand history lesson. Some of the most interesting conversation centered on the word "swear" (which was

a definite "no-no" to young Piedmont Triad folks in 1953). The teacher explained that the constitutional language gave the option to "affirm" instead of "swear." And Sunday school scholars knew that Matthew 5:34–35 clearly noted, "But I say unto you, Swear not at all; neither by heaven; for it is God's throne: Nor by the earth; for it is his footstool."

What we didn't expect at the time of President Eisenhower's 1953 inauguration was his July 16, 1956 organization of the President's Council on Youth Fitness after his learning from a study that American youth were less fit than European youth.

Almost one month to the day before Ike's inauguration, Amy Jo Younts, a resident of Arcadia and a ninth-grade student at the new North Davidson High School, was privileged to have this essay published:

WHAT I EXPECT OF THE NEXT PRESIDENT OF THE UNITED STATES

Because so many people at home and abroad are concerned with the government of these United States, and because the president is the head of the government, I as a citizen of the United States expect certain high qualities of leadership.

First I expect honesty. Without honesty a leader cannot gain the respect and confidence of the people. A man who is sincere and truthful will have cooperation of the people. In order to have success he must have cooperation.

Next I expect a man who does not seek personal gain, but one who seeks to benefit all the people. A man who has the welfare of the people at heart will understand their problems, the farmer, the laborer, the businessman, and the housewife. All have equal rights in this democracy of ours.

Because there has been much communist activity in this country I expect a man who will fight communism. Communism is a threat to the American way of life. People under such a government have no freedom of speech, religion, or press—the things we value most.

Above all I expect a president who will look to God for strength to guide us toward peace and prosperity for all mankind.

If the president of the United States has these important qualities, then "government of the people, by the people, and for the people shall not perish from this earth."

Golden School Days

Elementary school days were different back then. Children did not change classes or have physical education classes, homerooms, sex education or thoughts of crime. Practically every boy carried a pocketknife in his pocket. Nobody ever got hurt or even threatened. It was just that simple; that's what boys did. On the other hand, peashooters were banned. Having a weapon in school meant being caught with a slingshot. The school morning started with devotions in each and every classroom, first through seventh grade. The teacher (always female) read a daily Bible story, we repeated the Lord's Prayer and occasionally we sang the first verse of a well-known hymn.

We had both a morning and afternoon recess. Boys played baseball (with no adults to help them with the rules of the game) on the big lot behind the school building. Their worst embarrassment was being picked last for a team, so sometimes they used the "eeny, meeny, miney, moe" selection method. Girls stayed on the front lawn and exercised with a game of kickball, jump rope or hopscotch. Never the two genders would meet! Lunch in the cafeteria was delicious. Everything was homemade: meat loaf, mashed potatoes, mac and cheese, hot yeast rolls and apple or cherry cobbler. The cost was twenty-five cents per day. Teachers ate at one long table; they never had to interrupt their meal at any time to discipline anyone. After lunch—called "dinner" in the Piedmont Triad—kids could visit the school store and purchase ice cream in little pop-top cartons, candy cigarettes or wax Coke-shaped bottles with colored sugar water inside.

The highlight of each school year was the nomination of student officers. Young candidates adorned the hallways with handmade posters announcing their qualifications. The week of elections, everyone gathered in the auditorium, sang a few songs from *The Golden Song Book* and then listened attentively as each candidate gave his or her campaign speech. Their pleas were genuine and rehearsed to the utmost. Everyone applauded respectfully. Usually, those students who presented the most original speech won the election.

Kids being sent to the principal's office was nothing compared to the fate that awaited them at home. They feared for their lives, but it wasn't because of drive-by shootings, drugs, gangs and the rest. Their parents and grandparents were much bigger threats! But they survived because their love was greater than the threat. After school officials first threatened to keep kids back a grade if they failed. Teachers and principals then did not promote them and did not explain or apologize for making them repeat a grade. Junior high Piedmont Triad students—supervised by their teachers and volunteer parents—usually made day trips to Chapel Hill, where they attended the planetarium in the morning and the (now) University of North Carolina campus in the afternoon. This visit to the campus often inspired eighth graders to set their sights on attending college there.

Family Reunions and Summer Hymn Sings

Summer family reunions, when clans gathered at various churches in the Piedmont Triad, began with a morning program, followed by a picnic lunch spread in the church hut on the grounds. Tables were laden with fried chicken, country ham, stewed beef, a medley of vegetables and several tables filled with homemade coconut cakes, cobblers and a variety of pies. An hour of fellowship and relaxation followed, during which old acquaintances were renewed and new faces introduced. The afternoon program usually began at about 2:00 p.m. with special quartet groups singing. That was followed by an invited guest speaker's message, a tribute to all deceased members in a memorial service and, finally, a business session. Some clans gave special awards to outstanding members. Everyone left renewed and full and happy.

Hymn singing events occurred throughout the summer months at various churches in the Piedmont Triad. At these, men, women and children joined in an hour of singing old favorite hymns.

Classic Department Stores and Krispy Kreme Doughnuts

Greensboro and Winston-Salem had glorious department stores in the 1950s. A few of them are still with us; others we remember as tangible parts of our shopping experiences. Thalhimers in Greensboro was a seventy-eight-thousand-square-foot building at 203 South Elm Street. The Winston-Salem store, which had seventy-five thousand square feet, was located at 500 West Fourth Street. Downtown store directories differed according to the number of floors. The main floor sold jewelry, handbags, gloves, hosiery, cosmetics, fragrances, stationery and books. What was often called the "Homemaker's Floor" displayed china, silver, gifts, table linens, sheets, blankets, curtains and housewares. The fashion department displayed sportswear, dresses, coats, millinery, fur, lingerie and bridal gowns. Infants', toddlers' and girls' wear occupied yet another department. An old directory also indicated a separate department for men's and boys' clothing, as well as accessories.

Montaldo's in Greensboro and Winston-Salem had basically the same store layout and sold upscale clothing, furs and designer shoes. These two stores also offered complete bridal services. A tearoom and delicatessen shop gave shoppers a place to relax after an afternoon of shopping.

Interestingly, Louise Thomas, who worked as a buyer for Thalhimers in 1959 in downtown Winston-Salem, wrote a book entitled *Dear Emily: A Memoir, My Life in the Fine Stores*. She explores her work at the store during its heyday. She was the first female officer of Thalhimers as a vice-president of the store, but she wrote of encountering a bit of male chauvinism outside the store. One reviewer of her book commented: "[It] leads me to offer this thought. Yes, in some ways things were pretty nice in downtown Winston-Salem…but women and blacks were still second-class citizens."

After shopping in Winston-Salem for hours, it was a real treat to drive to Krispy Kreme for a hot glazed doughnut…or maybe an entire box to take home. Today, Krispy Kreme products are sold over the entire Piedmont Triad. However, in the good ol' days, folks went to one store in a rented building on South Main Street in Winston-Salem in what is now called historic Old Salem.

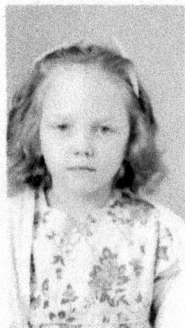

School Days
1944-45

School Days
1944-45

School Days
1944-45

Do You Remember These?

Previous, top: When black canvas baby carriages were deep and had tremendous handlebars? *Courtesy of author.*

Previous, bottom: When elementary school pictures looked like mug shots? *Courtesy of author.*

Above: When metal baby strollers were popular and huge boxwood hedges separated yards? *Courtesy of author.*

Right: When little boys wore suspenders to hold up their trousers? *Courtesy of author.*

PART IV

Hard Times

WORKING IN MILLS AND FACTORIES

Author Victoria Byerly explained, in poignant language, her personal interest in the men and women who worked in a Piedmont Triad cotton mill. She went back to her great-grandmother and great-grandfather to show readers their plights and their poverty:

> *Mary Frances was a good Christian woman and the mother of twelve children. My great-grandfather Cicero was a hard-working, hard-drinking man who nourished his family on the harvest of his rented land and nourished his spirit on corn liquor...Mary Frances was middle aged when she gave birth to her last child and she finally gave up on Cicero. She and the children moved to town and she went to work in the new Amazon Cotton Mill. Eventually all ten of her surviving children followed her to the Amazon, as did their children and their children's children.*
>
> *My grandmother Iola Mae married my grandfather Lacey at age fourteen, three years after she had gone to work in the Amazon. Like Cicero, Lacey was a hard-working man who loved his family but, also like Cicero, his love of corn liquor was what did him in. He was killed in a drunken brawl over the profits of a moonshine haul in 1948.*
>
> *Six months after he died, my mother, Clara Mae, gave birth to me. She was seventeen.*

Hard Times

When I went to work in the mill in 1967, four generations of women in our family had, all together, worked around four hundred years in the mill.

How did Victoria Byerly come to write a book about the hardships of women in Thomasville's Amazon Cotton Mills? She had been the first one in her family to graduate from high school and earn a scholarship to attend college, and she knew that she "wasn't meant for the mill." She walked out, thinking that she would never return; however, when she was a twenty-nine-year-old unemployed young woman, she returned to the Amazon Cotton Mill village and lived with her grandmother. Byerly began interviewing hundreds of millworkers and came to realize their struggles through their life stories. These she recorded in her book and are recorded here:

BERTHA AWFORD BLACK: I was the seventh child. We all went to work in the Amazon Cotton Mill and we all worked there all our lives. We lived over there right in front of the old drugstore beside the cotton mill. The mill had three-room and four-room houses, so we moved into a four-room house. I was eleven and my sister was ten when we went to work in the mill. The girl that trained me was younger than that. I stayed with her, her a-learning' me, for about two weeks, and I didn't get nothing for it. Not while I was a-learning. Then they put me on two sides, two spinning frames, and I made twenty-five cents a day. We went in at six in the morning and got out at six at night. And we worked Saturdays. I worked two weeks and my first payday I drawed $2.50. After a few weeks' time I got to where I could run six sides. That was seventy-five cents a day and I drawed nine dollars for a full payday every two weeks. I'd take that money and I'd give it to our mother. We all did, because she raised the family, bought our food and clothes. That thar child labor law was wonderful when it came in.

CLARA THRIFT: In 1950, when my baby was a year old, I went to work at the Carolina Underwear Company. My job was called bar-tacking, and I worked as hard as I could to make production, which paid eight dollars a day. That first day, I went in and I was scared to death. I was so nervous, I felt like I couldn't do it, but then I knew I had to. Bar-tacking is sewing the seams in ladies' underwear. I'd turn the panties wrong side out and tack 'em up. If they were little girls' panties, I'd tack on little bows. I learned to work fast, real fast.

They kept the production quota real high. If anybody made any money, what I mean is making over production, they'd send a quality control man around to time you. Then they'd up production and tell everybody else, listen, they doing such and such, so you got to do such and such. They made sure you didn't make more than a dollar or two over production. I had to stick with it because I needed the money, but oh God, did I hate it.

The man I worked for there, the overseer, treated women bad, very, very bad, like they were stray dogs.

At the time I didn't think my work was dangerous but looking back now I realize it was, breathing in all that lint. The worse thing that ever happened to me was one night I was working and I just happened to look up and they had a sliding door and my best friend was sitting there, she was the one who carried the yarn to weigh it up. I looked up, just happened to, and I seen that huge door falling and I hollered. She jumped up and ran toward me because she thought I had hurt myself. And when she did, the door fell right where she had been. It was a huge old door and if it had fallen on her it would have crushed her sure as the world. That was like a nightmare.

Then Daddy died. Drunk, he and his uncle got in a fight over some moonshine they had been hauling, and Daddy got shot in the head. He was no more than buried when I found out that I was pregnant. Mama was at her wits' end and she beat the hell out of me when she found out. From then on I was kind of a marked woman.

ALIENE WALSER: My mother died when I was five, my father died when I was six, and I was switched here and yonder and everywhere. My mother's sister was mainly responsible for raising me. There were thirteen children in her family—three girls and ten boys. She kept me from the time I was five years old until I was ten. Then she said she couldn't keep me no more. Well, they brought me over here to the Baptist orphanage and tried to put me in that orphanage home. But they said my mother and father had died of tuberculosis, so they wouldn't take me…So I went to stay with my grandmother and I stayed there about a year before she said that she couldn't keep me.

Finally, when my brother got married, I came to live with them. His wife and him separated when I was fourteen years old, so I quit school and went to housekeeping for this family who had four children. Two dollars a week for cooking and scrubbing. That's when I met my husband Anderson. Me and Anderson went to Virginia to get married. He was seventeen and I was fourteen, but Anderson told them in Virginia that he was twenty and that I was eighteen. I didn't weigh but seventy-four pounds. Well, the magistrate looked at us and he said, "You younguns go home." So we come back home and his mother and one of his aunts signed for us, and we got our license.

Preacher James out on Fisher Ferry Street married us. That night, I'd say we married about one-thirty in the afternoon, at four o'clock he went in to work at the mill. Then we lived with his parents in a mill house right behind the mill. When I was pregnant for the first time, I was sitting there sewing with my mother-in-law one night and I said, "I wouldn't mind having this baby if I didn't have to have my stomach cut open." She looked at me and said, "Honey, you mean that you don't know no better than that and fixin' to have a baby?" I said, "What do you mean?" And when she told me I said, "Ain't no way I'm going to go through that." That like to have scared me to death.

Broadus Mitchell, professor emeritus of economics at Rutgers University, gave the history of child labor in mills a different slant. He explained his position in his book, *The Rise of Cotton Mills in the South*: "The use of children was not avarice then, but philanthropy; not exploitation, but generosity and cooperation and social-mindedness."

MEN AND FAMILIES GO TO FORT BRAGG DURING WORLD WAR II

On December 20, 1945, two groups of Piedmont Triad men were sent to Fort Bragg. One group of ten reported for pre-induction examinations and another group of twenty for induction into the armed services. All thirty inductees' names were listed in the December 6, 1945 newspapers.

My father, mother and I were in Fort Bragg until the end of the war. We lived in a barracks-like apartment on Honeycutt Circle. My father trained mechanics during the day. My mother and I stayed at home, and I played with other children living in the complex. We had a living room and kitchen downstairs. On the second floor, we had one small bathroom and three tiny bedrooms: one for my parents, one for me and one that we rented to the wife of a Fort Bragg soldier who stayed on the army base.

On Sunday afternoons, my father took me to a nearby park to play with the other army brats. We always—without exception—had to be home by six o'clock in the evening to listen to Edward R. Murrow's news broadcast on the radio.

Above: The Fort Bragg Ordnance Motor Repair Shop was where soldiers maintained and repaired army vehicles at the northwest corner of Macomb and Sturgis Streets in Fayetteville, North Carolina. *Courtesy of Library of Congress.*

Left: The road to Fort Bragg Military Reservation directed World War II soldiers and their families to their temporary wartime residences. *Courtesy of Library of Congress.*

The author's Fort Bragg home during World War II. The barracks-like apartment was primitive and small, but there were lots of children to play with. *Courtesy of author.*

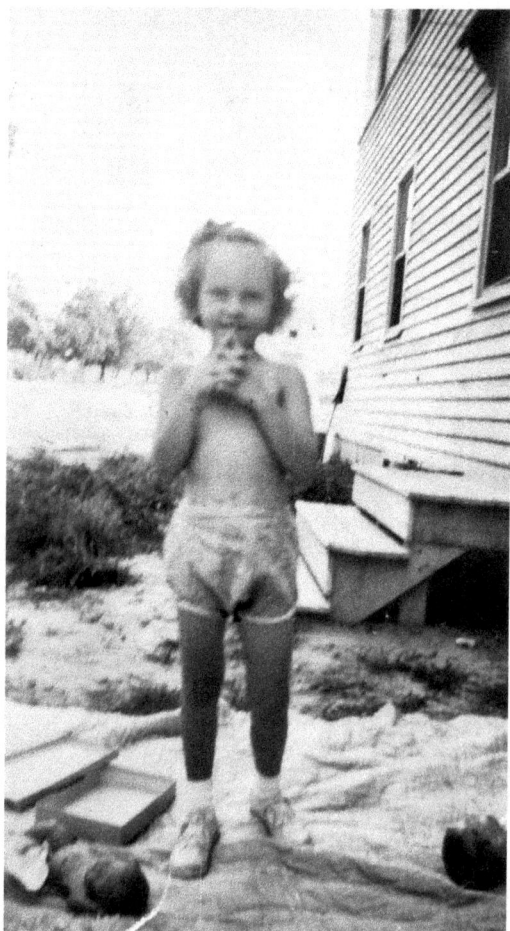

Above: World War II photograph taken outside crude Fort Bragg apartment. *Courtesy of author.*

Left: The author playing in the backyard at the Fort Bragg apartment during the war. *Courtesy of author.*

The author with her father and mother at Fort Bragg, all dressed up, outside the apartment building. *Courtesy of author.*

We attended what I now think was a Baptist church not far from where we lived. On our first visit, my parents left me in the nursery while they attended the 11:00 a.m. worship service. When they came back to collect me at noon and take me home, the nursery attendant told them, "Your daughter certainly entertained us this morning by standing on the table

Sugar rationing proved to be a fair exchange for all Americans during World War II. Coupons from the war ration books ensured a just distribution of the nation's sugar supply to all. *Courtesy of Library of Congress.*

and singing 'Pistol Packin' Momma.'" I don't think we returned for another church service.

Wartime definitely affected the area. Sugar rationing was implemented. Women's silk stockings were unavailable, so ladies began to apply leg makeup. Gasoline was difficult to obtain. In general, World War II took its toll. When we had enough gasoline to drive back to the Piedmont Triad for an occasional weekend or special holiday, we always had Fort Bragg soldiers crammed in the rumble seat of our old car.

Years later, I learned that one of my high school teachers was one of those soldiers riding in the rumble seat. Small world!

BOARDINGHOUSES BECAME POPULAR AFTER GREAT DEPRESSION

In the early 1940s, the Piedmont Triad began recovering from the Great Depression. In many towns, mills and factories were reopened, so men and women looking for work left their homes and migrated from neighboring rural areas. They needed a place to live.

Widowed women opened their homes to these workers. The typical residence—a large, unheated two-story house—could accommodate as many as a dozen paying guests. The downstairs most often consisted of a dining room, kitchen and the family's living quarters. The upstairs usually had four bedrooms with as many as three double beds in each—always two people to one bed. One bathroom at the end of the hall contained a toilet, a sink and a tub; occasionally, there was no hot water. The cost to these textile workers was three to four dollars per week. This included three bountiful meals a day, served family style. Boarders helped themselves to bowls filled with vegetables, platters of meat and baskets of homemade biscuits, all placed in the center of the table—hence the regional term "boardinghouse reach" because men were notorious for reaching across the table to fork the last piece of chicken or biscuit.

Boardinghouse history provides a nostalgic note to the author of this book. My Grandmother Evans ran a boardinghouse within walking distance of all the factories and mills in Lexington. Jenny Alice Wood Evans's backyard

Grandmother Evans's big boardinghouse (back left) and the author's Lexington, North Carolina homeplace (back right). Robbins School football players are in foreground. *Courtesy of author.*

Grandmother Evans with granddaughters Alice and younger sister Ann, seated on a couch at Uncle Harold and Aunt Mary Noble's house in Welcome, North Carolina. *Courtesy of author.*

adjoined ours. Her house stood tall and boxy and unheated. The downstairs living room remained unused and cold except on Christmas Day, when a space heater gave out intermittent heat for our family gathering.

My grandmother's bedroom held her double bed, sagging with the same mattress that had served as a birthing place for her five children, one of whom was my father. A dresser with an antique mirror and an overstuffed chair completed the furnishings. Her small bathroom contained a commode, a lavatory and a tub that, for some reason or another, never worked and became storage space for suitcases and extra blankets. She bathed at the small sink with water heated in a pot on the kitchen's wood stove and carried to the bathroom.

Grandmother's only female boarder, Blanche, occupied a downstairs front room with double French doors. I suppose she bathed and brushed her teeth at my grandmother's bathroom lavatory and used a slop jar during the night. I can see how, with careful scheduling, that sharing could have worked.

The dining room held a huge oak table, a dozen or more mismatched chairs, a sideboard, a china closet with her set of "Mildred" china (no paper plates for her) and, near the open fireplace, an easy chair, a radio and an overstuffed sofa. Her roomy kitchen contained both wood and gas stoves, a single-base enamel sink and a large table with a marble slab for cutting mints and rolling pie crusts. In a freestanding cupboard, my grandmother kept flour, sugar, spices and jars filled with saved string and recycled buttons. A refrigerator, chilling green quart jars of homemade buttermilk, stood in one corner. Between the dining room and kitchen, two large pantries held shelves loaded with vegetables—bell jars filled with green beans, beets, soup mixture, squash, butterbeans, corn and bread-and-butter pickles. A salted country ham hung from a large nail on the rafters.

The men who lived upstairs worked in local furniture factories or cotton mills. Blanche sewed at the shirt factory. They ate breakfast, dinner (the noon hour was signaled for all workers by one loud blast from the town's fire horn) and supper at my grandmother's seven days a week. She raised her own vegetables and chickens and made her biscuits and corn bread from scratch. Staples, which she ordered from Michael's Store just two blocks over, arrived at her house via a deliveryman, who entered her back door (usually without knocking), deposited everything on her kitchen cabinet and sometimes left without a word.

Born in 1940, I arrived during the last phase of my grandmother's boardinghouse days. By the late '40s, all the boarders had left. Other than Blanche, some specific memories have faded, but I'll always remember all those people eating chicken and dumplings at Grandmother's table or swaying in oversized rockers on her front porch.

POORHOUSES, COUNTY HOMES AND EARLY NURSING FACILITIES

Poorhouses were government-run facilities in the Piedmont Triad for the support and housing of dependent or needy persons. Typically run by various counties, these facilities housed the destitute elderly and were often called "shelters." Sometimes the poorhouse was situated on the grounds of a "poor farm" on which all able-bodied residents were required to work. Those who were too old or frail to labor were lodged in large rural houses. They had no responsibilities.

These poorhouses were also called "county homes" and were the only option for some indigent, elderly and disabled men and women. Today, those institutions have vanished. Poorhouses closed as communities found other ways to care for the needy. Others became nursing homes or juvenile detention centers.

The 1950 amendments to the Social Security Act created a significant change in the way that welfare was delivered and paid for: "The Federal Government will share in cost of payments made directly to medical practitioners and other suppliers of medical services, which when added to any money paid to the individual, does not exceed the monthly maximums on individual payments."

Nursing home operators could now contract directly with the states for payment, providing nursing homes with a new and more reliable source of income. In 1956, the Social Security Act was again amended to eliminate

Youth fellowship social at High Rock Lake following our presentation of a Christmas program to folks at the county home. *Courtesy of author.*

that cap. This was extremely important because nursing home costs were much higher than the individual payment. The elimination of the cap on payments meant that the government quickly became the primary purchaser of nursing home care.

In the '40s and '50s, church youth groups and their advisors presented Christmas programs at various county homes. Residents were bathed and neatly dressed for visitors. They sat in straight-back chairs lined against three walls of a large front room. A piano stood against the fourth wall. An anemic Christmas tree stood in the corner. Decorated with colorful paper loops and "snow" made from Ivory flakes and water, but no lights or ornaments, it was definitely one of those Charlie Brown images.

None of the residents responded as youth groups sang Christmas carols, accompanied on the out-of-tune piano by one of the more talented young people. They sat there, muted and unemotional, as the Christmas scripture was read, more carols were sung and a closing prayer was offered. Occasionally, an attendant would straighten a resident in his or her chair, wipe a drooling mouth or pat a stooped shoulder. The conclusion of the youth fellowship visit consisted of presenting each person with a Christmas gift wrapped in bright paper and tied with a festive bow. Everyone was still silently seated while the youth group and advisor filed out of the house in single file, singing, "We Wish You a Merry Christmas and a Happy New Year." The next stop was at a cabin at High Rock Lake, where the group enjoyed a different type of party.

Do You Remember These?

Left: When every female dressed up for Easter Sunday? *Courtesy of author.*

Below: When it was savvy to join a music club, even if you couldn't carry a tune in a bucket? *Courtesy of author.*

Opposite, top left: Your first precious dog, of which you were so proud? *Courtesy of author.*

Opposite, top right: When little boys played with homemade airplanes? *Courtesy of author.*

Opposite, bottom: When girls wore skirts and blouses to school? *Courtesy of author.*

PART V
Strange as It May Seem

NEWSREELS ENTERTAINED MOVIEGOERS

People in the Piedmont viewed the news every week in their neighborhood movie theaters. Newsreels were shown before every feature. Universal Newsreel, produced in the '50s, was released twice a week. Each issue contained six or seven short stories, usually one to two minutes in length, covering world events, politics, sports, fashion and whatever else might entertain the movie audience. These newsreels offered fascinating and unique views of an era when motion pictures defined our culture and were a primary source of visual news reporting. By the 1960s, newsreels had lost their audience since more people were watching nightly news shows on television.

One particular newsreel filming company, News on the March, included a combination of pictures, background music and interviews. Here are two examples of narration, which were delivered in a booming voice:

A COUPLE IS KILLED AND THEIR CHILDREN ARE MISSING. COULD COMMUNIST UNION SYMPATHIZERS BE TO BLAME?

OAKLAND WOMAN'S ROWING GRANDMOTHERS CLUB HAS SEVENTY-THREE MEMBERS. THEY HAVE ROWED ONCE A WEEK FOR THIRTY-SEVEN YEARS.

During the month of December, movie theaters showed a series of "Christmas Brings Joy to Everyone" newsreels with shots from various areas of the United States.

The Possum in the Mash: Enough to Keep Anybody Sober

In a newspaper interview with Shelly Smith Graham when he was eighty-nine years old, he related to a reporter an unusual regional moonshine-busting experience.

"The worst one I ever saw," Graham said, "is they threw a possum in the mash." The moonshine setup with the possum in it was composed of four-hundred-gallon mash boxes. "And they put their mash in there, let it ferment," he said. "And one of them put a possum in the mash. He was floating in the mash when we got it. It just speeded up the fermentation." But the moonshiners never got to run that still, Graham said. "We just blew the possum up along with the still."

The southern mode of whiskey making involved the illicit distillation of liquor by men who gathered in the woods at night. *Courtesy of Library of Congress.*

Two men stand outside with their small still; one of them holds up a bottle of liquor. *Courtesy of Library of Congress.*

Another operation Graham found was underground, under a hog pen. "The hogs were just running around on top of it," he said. Heart attack hooch.

David Graham developed an unusual talent during his years hunting and destroying moonshine stills. He could shake a mason jar filled with the amber liquor, look at the bubbles coming to the top and predict the strength. "It's about 90 proof; the longer the beads, the higher the proof," he would state matter-of-factly. Then, after his guess, he shook the jar again, took off the lid, "dipped his index finger into the jar and had a taste," which confirmed his bubble test.

Graham was no stranger to Piedmont Triad moonshiners. One day, when the unit didn't have any pressing business, the men walked through the woods for several hours. "We found five stills," Graham said, laughing. "We took an axe with us and chopped them all up. That was a lot of fun back then, I'll tell you that. We had something to do every day."

GASOLINE RATIONING IN 1942

The year 1942 was a time of strict gasoline rationing, as reported in a May 7, 1941 newspaper article entitled "Hargrave Heads Gas Rationing for District." A total of sixty-one thousand forms would be used in gas registration in Davidson County. These would be divided proportionately between Thomasville and Lexington. Principals of separate grammar schools serviced as administrators. Teachers and town citizens acted as assistants. These were the rules:

> In order to register for gas ration cards, it will be necessary for each vehicle owner, with exception of certain classes such as plainly marked governmental cars, trucks, buses, etc. to present his motor vehicle registration card. He will then answer necessary questions on the number of "essential" miles he may cover in going to and from work. Five different types of rationing cards will be issued. The amount of gasoline given each motorist will be based on the importance of himself and his vehicle to the present war emergency. Basic ration cards "A" are expected to be the largest number issued. They are the type issued to average citizens.

The article continued, covering all possible bases for misuse. Citizens were instructed to register the make, model and type of car they operated and also give the license and motor numbers before any gasoline cards would be issued. In addition, cards could not, in any circumstances, be transferred, "meaning that even if a car owner is traveling with a friend, that gasoline intended for one vehicle may not be bought for another." Actual gas rationing was scheduled to get underway on May 15, 1942. After rationing was over, "filling stations," as they were called back then, competed with one another by having gas wars, and gasoline sometimes dropped to eleven cents a gallon.

SCHOOL BOMB HOAXES AND TELEPHONE THREATS

The year 1958 brought school bomb hoaxes to the Piedmont Triad. Telephone calls warning of bombs planted in schools were reported in both Winston-Salem and Asheboro. Winston-Salem Columbia Heights elementary and junior high schools and Northwest High School in the county were evacuated after telephone calls were made declaring that bombs were in the buildings. Two threats were called in to Reynolds High School and also Wake Forest College. The Winston-Salem Chamber of Commerce posted a $1,000 reward for the capture of anyone making the bomb reports.

The bomb threat at Asheboro High School was thought to be a prank played by a student; nevertheless, all students were dismissed from the building. Chief of Police Clarence Lovett gave the following information: "He received a telephone call at 8:05 a.m. The voice on the phone was described as that of a 'youthful male.' The voice said, 'A bomb has been placed in the high school building to go off in about six hours. Thank you.'"

After a thorough search of the high school, police found nothing. Chief Lovett said that he thought the call was "some childish prank."

PALMISTS AND ADVISORS: NO APPOINTMENT NEEDED

The 1950s in the Piedmont Triad produced appearances of palmists and advisors who promised to give never-failing advice on all matters such as courtship, marriage and business speculations. Madame Lou Lou, Madame Christine or Madame Viola promised that they would lift you from your trouble and start you on the path of prosperity.

You were guaranteed sound advice for happy marriages or solutions for lovers' quarrels, evil habits and bad luck. These readers believed that there was "no heart so sad or home so broken that I cannot bring sunshine to." No appointment was necessary, and readings—for "White and Colored" alike—were strictly confidential. Several techniques surrounded palmistry:

Chiromancy consists of the practice of evaluating a person's character or future life by "reading" the palm of that person's hand. Various "lines" and "mounts" purportedly suggest interpretations by their relative sizes, qualities, and intersections. In some traditions readers also examine characteristics of the fingers, fingernails, fingerprints, and palmar skin patterns, skin texture and color, shape of the palm, and flexibility of the hand.

A reader usually begins by reading the person's dominant hand (the conscious mind). The other hand is subconscious (believed to carry hereditary or family traits or convey information about past-life).

Each area of the palm and fingers is related to a god or goddess, and the features of that area indicate the nature of the corresponding aspect of the subject. For example, the ring finger is associated with the Greek god Apollo; characteristics of the ring finger are tied to the subject's dealings with art, music, aesthetics, fame, wealth, and harmony.

Those who practice chiromancy are generally called palmists, palm readers, hand readers, hand analysts or chirologists. Sometimes palmists were located in a trailer at a service station. A sign with an open palm reaching toward the moon signaled a reader's exact location.

"Hot" News from Asheboro

Folks in the Piedmont Triad were delighted to learn in January 1954 that the reputable General Electric Company was making electric blankets in a big Asheboro plant that was originally built for a furniture factory. Rumor had it that about five hundred people would be employed in this plant. Asheboro was strong in textiles and furniture, but its business leaders were also diligent in their effort to attract industries of a more diversified nature. Electric blankets—what will they think of next, we all wondered.

Actually, what we did not realize in 1954 was the fact that the first crude electric blanket was invented in the early 1900s. They were big and bulky heating devices that were dangerous to use. By 1921, electric blankets were starting to receive more attention after being regularly used in tuberculosis sanitariums. Tuberculosis patients were routinely prescribed lots of fresh air, which included sleeping outdoors. The blankets were used to keep the patients warm. The first automatic electric blanket had a separate thermostat control that automatically turned on and off in response to room temperature, and it went on sale in the United States for $39.50. The name "electric blanket" was not used until the 1950s—the blankets used to be called "warming pads" or "heated quilts."

Infantile Paralysis Quarantines Children

At the time of the 1944 polio epidemic, Piedmont Triad youngsters were taken by ambulance or hearse (when ambulances were already in service) to the Emergency Polio Hospital in Hickory because other facilities were filled. Within fifty-four hours, a fresh air camp for underprivileged children had been turned into a working polio hospital. From Johns Hopkins Hospital

Visitors' Day, 1944–45, at the Emergency Polio Hospital in Hickory, North Carolina, where many Piedmont Triad children were taken for treatment. *Courtesy of Bett Hudson Eatman.*

came physical therapists and skilled doctors. Yale University sent research specialists. The July 31, 1944 issue of *Life* magazine published a story with pictures of the polio hospital. Research indicates that this was the first integrated hospital in the Southeast. The Emergency Polio Hospital closed in June 1945 after all the children were moved to a newly built wing at Charlotte Memorial Hospital.

Polio hit again in July 1948, and three new cases of infantile paralysis (polio) were reported to the office of Dr. G.C. Gambrell, Davidson County Health doctor, bringing the total number of cases in the county up to ten. Dr. Gambrell advised parents to keep their children under sixteen years of age away from all gatherings. Although he did not announce a general quarantine, he felt that individual cooperation would make the unofficial quarantine effective.

In several Piedmont Triad towns—including Greensboro, High Point and Thomasville—ordinances were passed that closed swimming pools and barred admission of children under sixteen to theaters, ballgames and other places such as Sunday schools. A total of 2,516 polio cases were reported in North Carolina, with no county having more people infected per capita than Guilford.

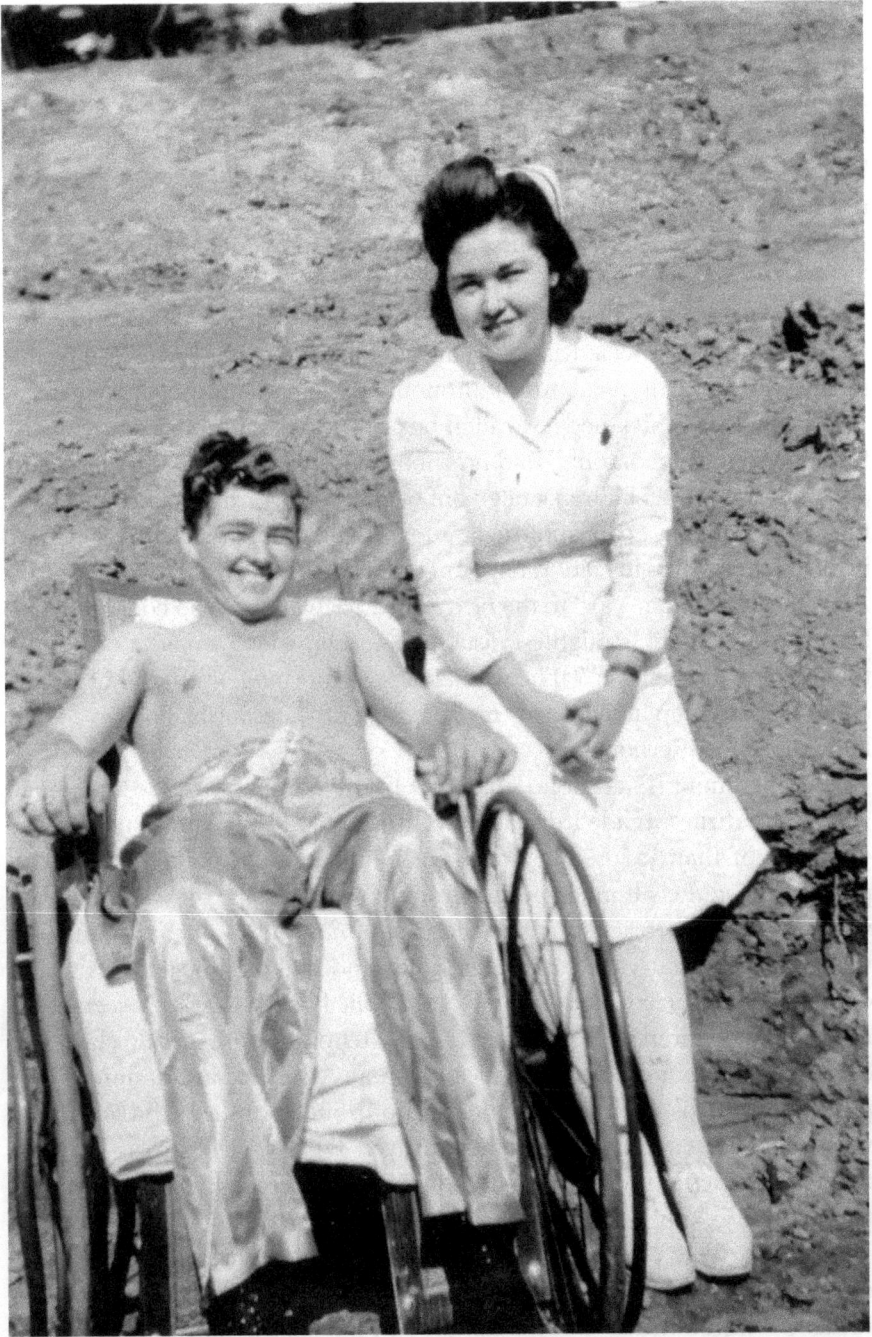

Nurse with her brother, who was a polio patient in 1944. *Courtesy of Bett Hudson Eatman.*

If a mother needed to drive to town for groceries or other needed goods, children could accompany her; however, they had to stay in the car with the windows rolled up. Remember that this was summer, so sitting in a vehicle with no air (no such thing as automobile air conditioning then) became extremely uncomfortable, to say the least. Waiting kids were often pacified with a Cherry Coke from Rexall Drug—that is, unless their mother happened to be a registered nurse (like mine) or proverbial know-it-all (also like mine) who swore that Coca-Colas actually *caused* polio. And how about the maternal instinct that said, "Hang cotton balls on your screen doors to ward off flies"—suspected all along, by many, to be the dreaded carrier of the terrible disease with the almost unpronounceable name of poliomyelitis.

Since tall and thick hedges, called box-bushes, often separated one yard from another in Piedmont Triad neighborhoods, children used their wits to get around the "no children can go out of their own yard" dictate. The boys took their miniature cars and trucks and, staying on their side of the hedge, involved themselves in elaborately conceived games involving "scooting" the toy vehicles from one yard to the next. The race was on. Who could send his little car the longest, straightest distance? And how long would it take for it to return to "home base"? The winner, after a morning or afternoon of this contest, got to keep his choice of his opponent's toy car stash! Then everyone had to take an afternoon nap.

The Piedmont Triad polio epidemic frightened parents. No one knew what caused the dreaded disease. Eventually, children were barred from going out of their yards. This was a curse on neighborhood children, who played during the summer months from dawn to dusk—moving from one yard to the next, constructing and acting as junior entrepreneurs, managing their summer front yard lemonade stands and making weekly trips to the dime stores, Saturday kiddie shows and public libraries. No one seemed to mind when children were prevented from attending confirmation classes or Sunday 11:00 a.m. worship services. For many, this was just an interesting postponement of their religious education, but for others, Bible lessons were taught over the radio. Planes sprayed DDT in the streets of most towns and cities in the belief that polio might be spread by flies, according to several accounts.

In the late 1940s, a makeshift hospital was set up in a recreation hall of the old Army Overseas Replacement Depot on Bessemer Avenue. Greensboro firefighters kept watch around the clock in case the ramshackle wooden building should catch fire. Dr. Gregory Revenel, Greensboro pediatrician, saw the need for a hospital. Within twelve days, he and local businessmen had raised $100,000 to build a facility on the (then) outskirts of the town, between Huffine Mill Road and Summit and Bessemer Avenues. The Polio Children's Hospital, as it was called, consisted of rows and rows of white cinder block buildings in which to quarantine children who had contracted polio.

Today, on this property in northeast Greensboro, a few buildings (now painted blue) with boarded windows remain—possibly as an abandoned monument. Over the years, the Polio Children's Hospital has been repurposed. In the 1950s, it temporarily housed students from nearby Bessemer School while it underwent renovation. The remaining structure is significantly smaller than the original. A "No Entrance" sign makes passersby wonder, "Just where was the entrance?"

When Every Home Had a Sears & Roebuck Catalogue

Some parents never owned their own home, never wore Levis, never set foot on a golf course, never traveled out of the country or had a credit card—unless they had something called a revolving charge card, good only at Sears & Roebuck. Or maybe it was Sears Roebuck. Either way, there is no Roebuck anymore. Maybe he died.

Parents never drove their children to soccer practice because no one had heard of soccer. Kids rode their bicycles around their neighborhood. The bike probably weighed fifty pounds and had only one speed (slow). There were pant leg clips for bicycles without chain guards.

All newspapers were delivered by boys who got up at 6:00 a.m. six days a week. Collection day was on Saturday, when they had to collect forty-two cents from each household. Favorite customers gave them fifty cents and told them to keep the change. Least favorite customers were the ones who never seemed to be home on collection day.

An old Royal Crown Cola bottle, filled with water, sat on the end of the ironing board. Its silver stopper had holes punched in it. This was to sprinkle clothes before ironing. No one had ever heard of a steam iron.

Cars had headlight dimmer switches on the floor and ignition switches on the dashboard. Drivers stuck their left arms outside the car window to give hand signals when they wanted to turn.

Fast food was unheard of for a long, long time. Folks ate at home. Mom cooked every day, and when Dad got home from work, everyone sat down

Note the glass milk bottles on the stoop. *Courtesy of author.*

together at the kitchen table. If kids didn't like what Mom put on their plates, they were forced to sit there until they did like it. Pizzas were not delivered, but milk was, in glass jars capped with cardboard stoppers. A mound of cream topped the contents of the full bottle. This was carefully spooned off and stored in the icebox until there was enough to make whipped cream. A woman from the country sold homemade buttermilk in green quart Bell jars. Women, even in the city limits, kept chickens enclosed in wire fences containing henhouses. These provided both eggs and fried poultry for the dinner table.

Sterling Silver Flatware: Beautiful, Sturdy and Inexpensive

Just about every young Piedmont Triad bride-to-be registered her choice of sterling silver flatware at her favorite jewelry store. A forty-two-piece set of Joan of Arc sterling sold for $79.50. Of course, few wedding guests could afford to pay this price, so they chose from one of the following pieces for the blushing bride:

- teaspoons, advertised at $13.40 per dozen (that's just over $1.00 dollar each)
- dessert spoons, advertised at $27.00 per dozen
- soup spoons, advertised at $29.00 per dozen
- dessert forks, advertised at $28.00 per dozen
- dinner forks, advertised at $33.00 per dozen
- iced tea spoons, advertised at $31.00 per dozen

Today, Joan of Arc by International Silver Company—currently in production—sells for much more: teaspoons are twenty to twenty-five dollars each, dessert spoons are twenty to thirty dollars each, cream soup spoons are twenty-two to thirty dollars each, dessert forks are twenty to twenty-five dollars each, dinner forks are thirty to forty dollars each and iced tea spoons are twenty to twenty-five dollars each.

Some jewelry stores engraved the bride's married initial on the silverware at no extra charge, gift-wrapped the package in exquisite silver foil paper with a big white bow and made personal deliveries, on a daily basis, to the bride's parents' home.

REXALL DRUG SPONSORED THE *JIMMY DURANTE SHOW*

Justin Whitlock Dar took control of Boston-based United Drug Company in 1942. The chain operated under the Liggett, Owl, Sonta and Rexall brands, which Dar rebranded under the Rexall name.

Rexall gained national exposure through its sponsorship of two classic American radio programs of the 1940s and 1950s: *Amos 'n' Andy* and *The Phil Harris–Alice Faye Show*. Both shows were often opened by an advertisement from an actor (like Griff Barnett) portraying "your Rexall family druggist" and included the catchphrase, "Good health to all from Rexall." Rexall also sponsored the *Jimmy Durante Show*, and there are references by the character Mr. Peavy in some of the *Great Gildersleeve* radio shows. Rexall also sponsored *Richard Diamond, Private Detective*, starring Dick Powell from April 1950 until Camel replaced Rexall as the sponsor after the December 6, 1950 broadcast.

By the late 1950s, Rexall's business model of unitary franchised stores, with each store owned independently by the local pharmacist, was already under attack by the discount chains such as Thrifty Drug and Eckerd. These well-financed corporate entities were able to drive down costs by means of block purchasing and were focused on growth.

Some of the deals Rexall Drug and Purcell's advertised on May 3, 1945, were as follows:

- Pinkham's Vegetable Compound—eighty-nine cents
- Castoria—twenty-four cents
- Phillips Magnesia—fifty-cent size for twenty-nine cents
- Sal Hepatica—forty-nine cents
- Feenament—nineteen cents
- 5-day Underarm Pads—fifty-five cents
- Tampax Sanitary Napkins—twenty-nine cents
- Petrogalar—All numbers—eighty-nine cents

Interestingly, items from the drugstore came without safety caps and hermetic seals because no one had yet tried to poison a perfect stranger.

Mann's Drug Store advertised popular brands of cigarettes for $1.64 a carton. And the NEW TONI TRIO customers could choose between three permanents for all different types of hair: Regular, for normal hair; Super, for hard-to-wave hair; and Very Gentle, for easy-to-wave hair. The price of each was $1.50, plus tax.

White versus Black Incidents Made Headlines

Making the front page of the *Dispatch* on December 6, 1954, was the following news story entitled "Conflicting Stories Told: Negro Boy Shot by White Youth":

> *Brodie Hairston, twelve-year-old son of Harrel Hairston, Negro of the Linwood section, was wounded seriously Sunday morning about 11:30, according to Deputy Sheriff Graham Leonard, who reports that the Hairston youngster was shot in the chest by a young white boy, also aged 12, whose name cannot be revealed since he is a minor.*
>
> *Deputy Leonard, who investigated the shooting on Linwood Road, said that an argument arose between the two boys, culminating when the white youth said he was going to go get his father's shotgun and kill the Hairston lad. On returning with a gun, according to the Hairston boy, the white boy shot him in the chest and arm, causing very serious injuries.*
>
> *The other boy involved told Deputy Leonard that the gun went off accidentally.*
>
> *According to Deputy Leonard, the Hairston boy had his arm in front of his chest at the time of the shooting, and his right hand was blown almost completely off. In addition, injuries to the youth's chest are reportedly very serious, and he remains in a critical condition today.*
>
> *Since he is a minor the name of the young white boy involved cannot be revealed for publication, but investigation into the matter is continuing, working to a determination as to what steps will be taken in the matter.*

Tales and Gossip: Thief at the Revival?

On the night of October 27, 1948, folks throughout Davidson County and possibly the entire Piedmont Triad attended a revival held by evangelist Charles A. Keyes. At the conclusion of this religious meeting, the organ used during the service, which belonged to Mr. Frank Shoaf of the Shoaf Appliance Company, was discovered missing. The following newspaper plea, which was not at all accusatory, did state that Mr. Shoaf had been "looking for the preacher and the organ," but the mystery was solved and given extensive coverage, as follows:

For the benefit of those who would like to have this falsehood verified, and save the preacher's reputation which is above reproach the following is what happened in regard to the borrowed organ at the close of the meeting. Evangelist Keyes borrowed a portable organ from Mr. Frank Shoaf to use during the last two nights of the meeting and understood that the organ would be returned Sunday night after the service.

Instead of Rev. Keyes returning the organ to Mr. Shoaf, a member of the Evangelistic Prayer Bank, Mr. Bill Logan, promised the evangelist he would deliver the organ Monday morning to Mr. Shoaf, due to the evangelist being tired in body and not familiar with the road to Mr. Shoaf's residence at night.

Here is what happened that has caused so much talk, concern, and misrepresentation, and discord since close of the meeting. Mr. Logan, who promised to assist the evangelist by delivering the organ, put same in his automobile Sunday night after close of service, saying he would deliver organ to Mr. Shoaf on Monday morning, but due to Mr. Logan's business, he failed to deliver the organ, and Mr. Shoaf, of course, didn't know what had become of the organ or the preacher until Mr. Logan turned up with same with his apologies for not letting him know he had the organ, and not the evangelist.

Mr. Frank Shoaf of the Shoaf Appliance Co. regretted that anyone who has heard the wrong thing or had the wrong impression of the evangelist and his organ, should contact him and he would clarify the matter.

The Morning Glory Café and the Famous Skeen Burger

In the '50s, folks in the Piedmont Triad loved (and still do) their famous barbecue sandwich, tray or salad. Another delicacy of the area was the Moose Burger—so called not because it was made from moose meat but because the restaurant that served it was the Big Moose. Imagine a Big Mac made with two-thirds of a pound of fresh ground meat, fresh lettuce, slices of Vidalia onion about half an inch thick, fresh buns and more.

Well, in Thomasville, they had their own burger claim to fame, the Skeen Burger, offered by the Skeen family. The restaurant (if you could call it that) was located near the railroad tracks, and every time a train came through, it shook the place. Skeen burgers were prepared only three or four ways, and a description was on a menu board and denoted just no. 1, 2, 3 or 4. Hungry folks sat on stools at the counter and ordered their choice. If they were famished, they just had to wait until Mr. Skeen, a retired barber, slowly and meticulously flipped burgers on his well-oiled grill. He charged thirty-five cents for each. He would not—and did not—hurry, so hungry customers waited patiently and listened to the trains go by outside. At about 3:30 p.m., Mr. Skeen hung up his apron, and he and his staff were gone for the day.

Word around the Piedmont Triad had it that Mr. Skeen once turned down a $10,000 offer for his recipe but later on sold it to a restaurant in High Point, North Carolina, called Der Shed. Reports were as you'd expect: "It was never the same." Maybe the mouthwatering wait while Mr. Skeen perfected his burgers made all the difference. We'll never know.

NIXON BLAMES GREENSBORO COLISEUM

Known originally when it opened in 1959 as the Greensboro Memorial Coliseum, less than a year later, presidential nominee Richard Nixon campaigned there. He received a knee injury and suffered a great deal of pain. Nixon's reaction to the accident was simple: "The first debate between John F. Kennedy and Nixon aired on television, with Nixon appearing to look 'sickly.' Nixon lost the debate and would go on to lose the presidential race. Nixon later stated the knee injury at the coliseum resulted in him losing the race."

FLYING SAUCERS

If *My Weekly Reader* printed it, fifth graders believed it! After all, this newspaper, published by the American Education Press, one of the oldest educational publishing houses in the United States, was required reading in many schools. The *Reader* for the September 18–22 week in 1950 carried an article by "Tom Trott," a frankly fictitious character, on flying saucers. Following is what "Trott" told us gullible kids:

This week we are at an airport on the Atlantic coast. The most exciting thing we have seen is "flying saucers."

For several years, people in many parts of our country have claimed to have seen flying saucers. The government proved that some of these people were imagining things. However, I am now allowed to tell you that some flying saucers are real. They belong to our Air Force. They will someday be a big help to our country.

My Weekly Reader went on to explain more about flying saucers: they were made in several sizes, the smallest being only six inches thick. The big ones might be as large as the width of five city lots. We fifth graders were also informed that these "strange objects" were made of material that dissolved after being in the air for a while. This is why saucers disappear soon after they hit the ground. We were also told that we would probably never find one, but if we should, we would find these words on it in black letters: "Military secret of the United States of America Air Forces." Then we received the following warning: "Anyone damaging or revealing description or whereabouts of this missile is subject to prosecution by the United States government."

Now, that is enough to frighten a fifth grader to death. Why, then, did the publishing house—which at that time had a fifty-year tradition of responsibility to the youngsters it served—publish such a story? One response came from the newspaper's managing editor, Miss Eleanor M. Johnson: "The staff is convinced that flying saucers most certainly are among this nation's experimental aircraft. Our correspondent had one idea in mind and that thought was to calm any hysterical fears some children might have built up from hearing too much talk about mysterious flying objects from other planets or deadly flying weapons of our enemies."

Yeah right! Was that really supposed to calm our hysterical fears?

EGG BREAKING PLANT OPENING SOON

Now this is a strange one. An egg breaking plant? The year was 1950, and an announcement came forth on January 14 that Lexington had just received notice from the State Employment Service that Standard Brands Inc. was going to open an egg breaking plant just as soon as new equipment could be installed. What? Equipment needed to break eggs?

Estimated employment was about two hundred people, and interested folks were instructed to apply at the State Employment Office. Finally, an announcement explained the purpose of the plant: the process of freezing fresh eggs.

No Big-Box Store

In the '40s and '50s, the Piedmont Triad had no big-box stores. Priddy's General Store in Danbury is one of the few mom and pop stores that has survived, having been in operation now for nearly 125 years. In fact, the store at the intersection of Sheppard Mill and Pleasant View Church Roads has been in the same building since 1888. The general manager and third-generation proprietor, Jane Priddy Charleville, invites visitors to "take a journey into the past where time stands still."

Practically everything in the store was made in America, with a goal to have many local items—such as homegrown tomatoes, onions, fresh peaches and peppers, as well as a handmade ham and hoop cheese sandwich—served on a paper towel over a checkered tablecloth. Visitors today find the same kind of merchandise sold way back when: old-fashioned candy, country hams, hoop cheese, baked goodies, local honey and molasses and mouth-watering jams and jellies.

Flat irons, overalls, work boots, old-fashioned glass soda bottles, antiques, cast-iron cookware, cookbooks and old signs are also displayed. Then there is an old wooden cook stove and antique scales. It's all there, a trip down memory lane to the '40s and '50s, "where old times are never forgotten, time stands still and homemade fried apple pies beckon visitors."

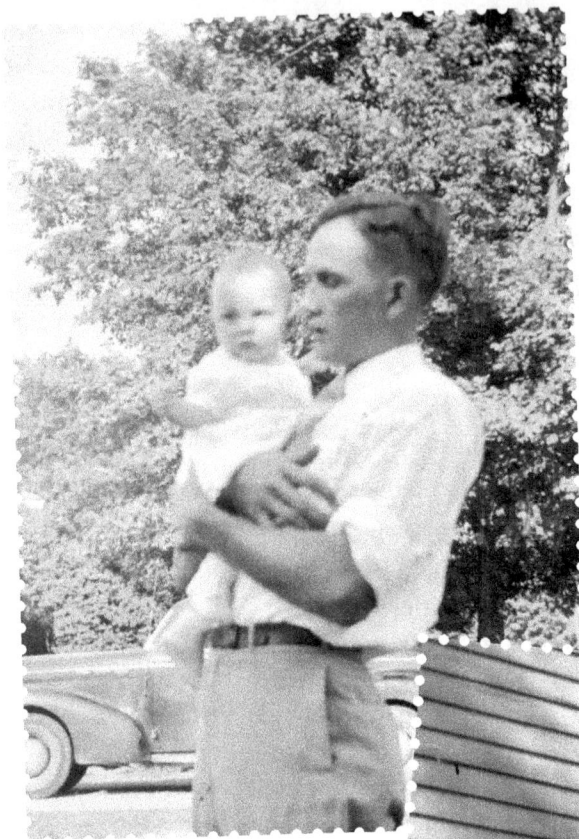

Do You Remember These?

Left: When families took Sunday afternoon car rides? *Courtesy of author.*

Below: When boys wore peg-leg pants? *Courtesy of author.*

Opposite, top: When boys wore knickers and babies sat in wooden high chairs? *Courtesy of author.*

Opposite, bottom: Family Christmas dinners with grandparents, parents, aunts, uncles and cousins? *Courtesy of author.*

PART VI
Amazing and True

The Glory Days of S&H Green Stamps

In the '50s, Piedmont Triad consumers, both men and women, liked to shop at stores that gave S&H Green Stamps. The retail organizations that distributed the stamps (primarily supermarkets, gasoline filling stations and shops) bought the stamps from S&H (Sperry and Hutchinson Company, founded in 1896 by Thomas Sperry and Shelly Hutchinson).

The stamps, issued in denominations of 1, 10 and 50 points, were pasted with a gummed reverse, and as shoppers accumulated the stamps, they moistened the reverse and mounted them in collectors' books, which were provided free by S&H. The books contained twenty-four pages, and to fill a page required 50 points, so each book contained 1,200 points.

Shoppers could then exchange filled books for premiums, including housewares and other items, from local Green Stamp stores or the S&H catalogue. Each premium was assigned a value expressed by the number of stamp-filled books required to obtain that item.

During the 1960s, the rewards catalogue printed by the company was the largest publication in the United States, and the company issued three times as many stamps as the U.S. Postal Service.

Interestingly, allusions to S&H Green Stamps appeared in popular culture. Stephen King attributes his first original short story idea to his mother's use of S&H Green Stamps. The unpublished "Happy Stamps" is about the counterfeiting of (the fictitious) Happy Stamps in order to purchase a house.

Don L. Lee published a poem in *Ebony* magazine that finished with the sentence, "Jesus saves, Jesus saves, Jesus saves—S&H Green Stamps." Pat Boone's hit "Speedy Gonzales" has as its last line, "Hey Rosita, come queeck, down at the cantina they're giving Green Stamps with tequila!" When adults took their cars to the "filling station," they got their windshield cleaned, oil checked and gas pumped, without asking, all for free every time. And they didn't have to pay for air. Then they got trading stamps to boot!

S&H was a pioneer in consumer loyalty and paved the way for credit card points and customer loyalty rewards.

No Dancing at Baptist Orphanage

Today, it's called Mills Baptist Children's Home, but in the '50s, the name was Baptist Orphanage, home to about 350 kids. This was the first children's home in the state of North Carolina and provided loving care to many Piedmont Triad youngsters. Estie Culler Bennington, age ten, went to live there from 1958 through 1966. She recalled her happy childhood experiences, as follows:

A social worker took me and my younger brother and sister to the Baptist Orphanage. I was assigned to a big house to live with 17 other girls my age in Biggs Cottage. We had a house mother who lived there 24/7 and a dietitian who also stayed there around the clock and cooked three meals a day. Favorites were meatloaf, fried chicken, and burnt sugar cake. Each girl was assigned a duty. Mine was to sweep the front porch. Other girls helped prepare the food and wash the dishes. Meals were served family style at tables seating four or five.

It was a huge house with many rooms. Two, three, or four girls shared bedrooms. We each had a twin bed, and we were taught how to make up that bed in military style. There was a bathroom between each bedroom. Sheets and towels were laundered once a week. Our clothes were sent to a central laundry room, but we washed our underwear in a washing machine in Biggs Cottage and hung them on an outside clothesline to dry.

At this time, boys lived on the opposite side of the campus, and their duties included working on the big farm. They had to get up about 5:30 in the morning to milk cows and do other chores. We girls were called to help in the summertime when the crops came in. We shucked corn in preparation for freezing in the Freezer Locker Room.

We went to different public schools, usually riding on the school bus; however those kids assigned to Colonial Drive School, walked the short distance. The eighteen girls in Biggs Cottage sat at the dining room tables and did our homework when we returned from our day at school. Church was a central part of everyone's life. We went to Sunday School, worship services, Vacation Bible School, and baptisms. We turned the one television on, tuned in "Dick Clark and American Bandstand," and did what we were not supposed to do—we danced! Crinolines, ponytails, braids, and

The audience prepares to dance on Dick Clark's *American Bandstand* television show. *Courtesy of theprincesandprincessesofdance.com.*

straight bangs were forbidden. We wore Sunday shoes, hats, and white gloves to church on Easter.

During summer vacation from school, we played in a big area called "The Valley." If we didn't have a big ballgame going, we'd swing, play on the monkey bars, skate (which required a key to tighten the skates on our shoes), or engage in a tennis match. We all loved to ride on one playground piece of equipment called "The Ocean Wave." When we rode, fire sparked out of the metal, and we delighted in that thrill. When I got older, we walked uptown to the Thomasville Diner, an old train car, for hamburgers or to one of the two theaters. Drive-in theaters were prohibited! Occasionally, we spent the weekend with the family of a girlfriend we had met at school.

Estie attends all Mills Home reunions and still stays in touch with her sixth-grade teacher. When Estie graduated from Thomasville High School in 1966, she left the home to be on her own and do her new job, but she always says that Mills Home shaped her life. She wrote and published a memoir of her days there.

NAT KING COLE AND ELLA FITZGERALD PERFORMED AT CLUB KILBY

This East Washington Street nightspot in High Point, Club Kilby, became a favorite Saturday evening hangout for adults. Patrons visited the downstairs bar before going up the wooden steps to dance and enjoy musical magic. Nat King Cole, who played only in clubs welcoming black people, crooned "Mona Lisa" or "When I Fall in Love" for the eager crowds. The Club Kilby rafters probably shook as Ella Fitzgerald, dubbed the "First Lady of Song," sang ballads or jazz in her flexible and wide-ranging voice. "Love and Kisses" brought clubbers to their feet.

To add to the famous list of entertainers, Edward "Duke" Ellington and his top-notch band offered favorites such as "Choo Choo, Gotta Hurry Home" and "Rainy Nights, Rainy Days." Billy Eckstine also added his magic to the entertainment lineup. The Furniture City Elks Lodge Ball spotlighted "Hartley Toots" and his orchestra.

Club Kilby closed in the early 1960s.

FUN AT THE "Y" WITH DANCES, FIGHTS AND ELVIS PRESLEY

A young Elvis Presley. *Courtesy of eftekasat.net.*

Friday night football games were followed by informal dances at the Young Men's Christian Association (YMCA). Kids fed the jukebox twenty-five cents and received five popular songs. Usually, at least one fight broke out between locals and out-of-town kids. Nothing more serious than a few rival punches ever occurred.

On March 21, 1956, Elvis Presley, touted as "one of the nation's great young Rock 'n' Roll stars of television, radio, stage, and recording fame," performed at the Lexington YMCA. In 1959, one newspaper article compared rock-and-roll singers to backwoods farmers doing hog calls. Elvis Presley, with his swiveling hips and sensual sneer, was one of the most controversial rock performers of the era. The Piedmont Triad area of North Carolina was one of his first stops. His appearance was complete with his intricate motions and his caressing and making love to his guitar as he swirled his hips—sparking adults' accusations of his "selling sex with cold, deliberate calculation." And the mothers in the audience were *shocked.*

He was paid $200 for his appearance. Franklin Young of the *Florida Times Union* recalled that event:

> *It was literally a bumpy road in the beginning, one of second hand Cadillacs and one-night stands during which screaming fans could crowd the bandstands within touching distance. Twenty years ago, this writer and a newspaper photographer traveled some 30 miles to catch one of Presley's earliest concerts. His name had just begun to flash across the country and within a matter of months was to become a household byword. Presley*

was playing another of those tiring one-nighters, this one in Lexington, NC. A national magazine had dispatched a writer, who kept shouting to this reporter over the ear-piercing screams of a surging mass of boby-soxers [sic]. This is unbelievable. Presley was so happy to get publicity in those days, the reporter was able to interview him throughout an intermission in his dressing room. Presley himself was so awed by the whole thing, he could hardly believe it. During one break, this newsman cornered one of the Presley group, a cousin attired uncomfortably in an ill-fitting dinner jacket, something he obviously was unaccustomed to wearing. The Presley's cousin, looking around in utter amazement, uttered, "This balloon is gonna burst."

Oh, what a tangled web that cousin wove!

Then, in August 1956, Piedmont Triad newspapers printed Hal Boyle's AP article entitled "Elvis Seen as Way to Educate Public on Sex." Boyle argued that Elvis Presley was "maybe the unrecognized hero of America's greatest present need—someone to restore sex to its proper perspective." He elaborated:

Presley, the Caruso of the teen-age crowd, is a young former truck-driver, known by both his admirers and detractors as "Elvis the Pelvis." Many music critics say Presley's lusty caterwauling is way below par. Elvis is perhaps even more renowned for his hip wiggles than his vocal cords, and these have brought him denunciation from ministers and parents, who say his wriggles are too "suggestive." Personally, I can't see this honest but rich young Tennessee minstrel as a national calamity. He may, indeed, turn out to be a national blessing.

What was Boyle's rationale for this statement? He believed that Elvis would be followed by many imitators with inspired writhing, and they would make sex look ridiculous. "Civilization has gone off its rocker in the matter of a misplaced emphasis on sex," Boyle stated. He added the following comments:

We live in a "sexbomb" age. A "sexbomb," in the entertainment world is a performer who gets by on animal allure rather than on artistic merit. This is the public to whom sex has become a travesty. It is the public that believes a man can win the girl of his choice if only he uses the right kind of hair tonic and get ahead in his job if he uses the right kind of underarm deodorant. It is the public that believes the way to a man's heart can be won by any girl if she uses the right kind of lipstick, the right dentifrice or goes to the right charm school.

Boyle concluded by arguing that the "sexbomb" field, previously dominated by women, had shifted to males; however, "after Elvis, nobody could make anything of sex but a comedy."

MOVE THAT TABLE: MAKING A MOUNTAIN OUT OF A MOLEHILL

Quite often, what we today would consider insignificant news events were published, and they subsequently made their way into the homes of Piedmont Triad citizens during the '40s and '50s. One such lengthy newspaper article, dated July 15, 1948, probably gave readers more than they wanted to know:

> *Whether a writing table in the post office lobby shall be moved a bit to the right or whether it will continue to stand in its present location and partially block traffic into the lobby is a problem that is now being pondered by officials having charge of the maintenance of Federal property.*
>
> *It isn't as simple as it might sound or even appear to the post office patron. A good many of these have perhaps been puzzled as to why the table had not been pushed a foot or so to the right, particularly when they have started into the lobby through the new front door arrangement and found someone standing at the end of the table to address a letter or card or do something else while almost blocking the right hand opening.*

So why had nothing been done? A veteran post office employee explained, "Why, it would probably cost at least a hundred dollars to move that table." An explanation continued, noting that two long bars ran from the pedestals of the table right down through the lobby floor, clear to the basement, where big taps were fastened on those bolts.

If the table were moved and fastened down in the same manner, the cost would be rather high and would make necessary other improvements and repairs on the building. Post office customers offered many suggestions for solving the problem that were published in the newspaper. One man suggested that the taps should be unscrewed, the table prized up and the long bolts destroyed with a hacksaw. All well and good perhaps! There was one other problem. Suggested solutions did not comply with regulations of the Treasury Department, which owned or furnished the buildings used for post offices. The saga continued with no immediate solution in sight.

In the South, we call such nonsense "making a mountain out of a molehill."

Amazing and True

"Tell Her She Looks Well and Strong"

It was customary during the '40s and '50s to include "Personal Notes" in Piedmont Triad newspapers. One such printed plea was for readers to acknowledge a certain woman's hospital stay: "Send her a card or letter, pat her on the back and tell her she looks well and strong and to hurry home. You know how to talk to sick folks. Tell her a couple yarns. She will like that."

Hospital admissions and dismissals appeared in many Piedmont Triad daily newspapers. Names and addresses were printed. Birth announcements appeared, complete with the new arrival's full name, as well as his or her parents, siblings and grandparents. The father's occupation was also given. Not mentioned was the first name of the mother who had carried the child for nine months. She was listed as Mrs. So-and-So (her husband's name).

Great detail was also printed when someone was injured in an automobile accident, and it was not unusual to print minute details to explain his or her injuries, such as broken ribs, a jaw injury, a severe facial bruise or a leg fracture. Details on the demolished car or cars completed the article.

Local newspapers also printed the names of those children who suffered from tonsillitis, measles, chickenpox, mumps and broken bones. Also reported were minor operations, pneumonia, colds, infected legs, sore throats, flu and stroke or paralysis. Details accompanying these ailments were as varied as the illnesses. The sick one is described as "indisposed," "not very well," "on the sick list," "undergoing tests," "resting very well," "doesn't seem to improve" or "getting along as good as could be expected."

Greensboro Open Welcomed Sam Snead, 1957

Doug Ford, newly crowned Masters champion, and Sam Snead, runner-up in the Augusta, Georgia classic, headed the field of about 130 as the first rounds were played in the $15,000 Greater Greensboro Open golf tournament in April 1957. According to one report, "Between them they have accounted for the last three Greensboro titles and Snead has won the tournament six times." Following are some of the golfing statistics:

Snead, who early in the winter announced a limited tournament program for the year, included this stop on his schedule—with good reason. The White Sulphur

Springs, W. Va. Veteran, 45 next month, won the inaugural Greensboro tournament in 1938. Since then he's won five more, including the last two.

In the last eight years Sam's record in Greensboro shows four victories, one second and three thirds or tie for third. In that period he's figured in three playoffs, winning two and finishing second in the other, a four-man affair.

Four eighteen-hole rounds were played over the par-seventy Sedgefield County Club.

MAKEUP TRENDS AND VINTAGE FASHIONS

In 1958, Ambrose Bierce wrote, "To men a man is but a mind. Who cares what face he carries or what he wears? But woman's body is the woman." And that includes her hair! In the 1940s and 1950s, women who had in earlier years removed the stuffing from their bodices and bound their breasts to appear young and boyish returned to the hourglass shape. Marilyn Monroe was considered the epitome of the voluptuous and fleshy (yet naïve and childlike) ideal. She taught women that "men would make passes at girls who wore glasses—even rich men."

The quintessential '50s married glamour girl was Lucille Ball, whose fashion sense was as rigorous as her acumen proved to be. Lucy's poodle haircut was perfect for the day—shorter but perfectly controlled by permanent and frequent trips to the beauty parlor.

Peaches and cream makeup replaced any previous vamp-styled pallor. Lips were rosy pink or red and welcoming; eyes were lined in mascara. Eyeliners also made an appearance at night, as well as pastel nail color and eye shadow colors in blue and green. Eyebrows were plucked thin and slightly high, "as if to underscore the naïveté of the woman below them." Dimples were revered but not freckles. Bangs often consisted of pin curls finger fluffed into a fringe. Women "looked like dolls when the girl next door for daytime became an elegant Parisian model by night."

One observer offers the following reasons for the fabulous "Nifty Fifties Trends":

The Nifty Fifties were a continuation of Forties femininity, with a little added paranoia. Those men left alive had come home from war. The unusual thing about WWI was that for the first time women's work had expanded to all sorts of jobs—not just teaching or nursing. Women had worked in munitions factories, shipyards, banks—everywhere a man had gone to war, a woman had taken his place. But when the war ended, the factories and industries employing women dismissed them en masse. Women were sent home—even the single ones, the widowed with children, the ones who wanted and needed to work. Many women were delighted to return to housework and wifehood after years of hard work and privation. Some were angry and hurt at the change from wage earner to housewife.

Soon, babies were created and born in enormous numbers. The Baby Boom forced the country into something resembling normalcy; after all, kids require diapers and kindergartens and puppies and homes in the suburbs.

The television hit series *Happy Days* dictated ideas concerning '50s fashions for teenage girls. They bought cashmere twin sets and poodle skirts for date night, conservative mid-calf-length dresses and simpler skirts or even blue jeans for home. Trends were definitely conservative. A casual ponytail, wrapped in a scarf, was favored for school and classes. A 1950s teen party theme might include the sock hop, with dancers wearing rolled-up jeans and penny loafers or vintage circle skirts and Oxford shoes.

Critics complained that women should not spend so much money or time on their appearance. Some clergy members preached sermons urging women to avoid personal vanity and to maintain their natural looks without using cosmetics or hair colorants. Attitudes were changing, however, and fashion and beauty were increasingly regarded as worthwhile pursuits. Mass media, the film industry and companies in the beauty business promoted these ideas. Popular songs even urged women to stay young and beautiful. Consequently, the beauty parlor was a significant part of American culture for many women.

Women with large noses were warned to watch what they did with their coiffures because hair pulled severely back from the face tended to emphasize the nose. This was especially true with a ponytail. Bouffant bangs became popular, and women's magazines printed the secret to achieving this new hairdo: "Roll a plump strip of cotton batting into a kerchief and tie it across your forehead. Comb your bangs over this pad and then set them with a hairspray. Let the spray dry, remove the pad, and comb lightly. It takes about ten minutes."

The beehive hairstyle, which became popular in the '50s, was achieved by "backcombing your hair [i.e., holding your hair with one hand and brushing from your hand toward your scalp], then hair spraying the heck out of it, and shaping your hair into a high mount on the top of your head."

In the good old days, charming young ladies made trips to the beauty parlor for permanent waves in preparation for that first day of school. The procedure was grueling: an outer space helmet sprouting heated clips activated the "processing" on permanent rollers saturated with foul-smelling solution.

Perhaps girls and women should have heeded Marilyn Monroe's '50s philosophy: "Real glamour, it's based on femininity. I think that sexuality is only attractive when it's natural and spontaneous…We are all born sexual creatures, thank God, but it's a pity so many people despise and crush this natural gift."

SECRETS TO ACHIEVE CHARM IN 1950

One newspaper had columns entitled "Secrets of Charm" and proclaimed to women, "No back can be beautiful with sharp, wing-like shoulder blades." The solution was proclaimed as follows:

Exercise can't correct sharply protruding shoulder blades—not if you persist in carrying your shoulders incorrectly. If the back you turn to your public is to be beautiful, smooth, and wingless, be on guard against hunching when you sit, stand, and walk. The shoulder blades are two almost flat bones which attach to the shoulder points and spine by strong muscles. These muscles stretch and stay stretched if you habitually strain your shoulders forward. They become so weak, they cannot hold your shoulder blades flat, as Nature intended.

The article went on to instruct women on the solution to wing-like shoulder blades by checking their body alignment. Once a woman learns how to set her shoulders, the most important thing is to keep them that way at all times. The position, milady is informed, will be easier to hold, however, if for a while she does the following exercise routine daily: "Sit with your hips flat against a wall, so your elbows are close to your waist and the backs of your hands are flat against the wall opposite your shoulders. Now slide your arms up as far as they will reach, elbows and hands still touching the wall. Pull and stretch 10 times a day at first and increase to 30 times."

Cosmetic companies did not shy away from using good old-fashioned fear as a motivator for purchasing their products: "Should you not buy Dorothy Gray Solon face cream, your husband will leave you for another woman and you will die alone." This tragedy is compounded by the fact that nothing they had back then actually worked. The only thing that prevented millions of wrinkly women from being abandoned in favor of their smooth-skinned counterparts was the fact that divorce was more than frowned on and not quite so easy as it is today.

Women were advised by Elizabeth Arden which lipstick and nail polish to wear with certain garments. Following was the definitive guideline:

School House Red, Canary Red	*Light brown and green; reds & orange, black & white*
Rose Natural, Red Feather, Victory Red	*All colors but black and white*
Radiant Peony, Red Cactus	*Black and white, wine, royal blue and gray*
Crimson	*White, navy, and pastel evening colors*
Sky Belle Pink, Paradise Pink	*All pastels for day and evening*
Redwood	*Golden brown, forest brown, rust, olive, tangerine, slate blue*

Sears catalogues advertised the company's "Sensational Cosmetic Discovery: Help You Retain Younger Skin Beauty—Almost Overnight." A popular new beauty product in 1959 was TIME OUT, "which coaxes the return of teen age texture to aging complexions. Contains wonderful new moisture control lotion which performs miracles on exposed skin areas." TIME OUT was advertised as "POTENT!" With "one little dab containing Natural Moisture Factor 100% applied at night seeps in—sets up a moisture factor, which helps you regain a more youth-like complexion while you sleep." In addition, this product was touted as "never greasy, never messy, its delicate fragrance surrounds you with a spring-like halo while it creates a satin-smooth *feel* under your make-up."

CRAVING LEXINGTON BARBECUE

Lexington provided high school students an opportunity to walk to Stamey's Barbecue during their lunch hour. If anyone had a car, we'd beg a ride. Stamey's was uptown, on a corner across from the side of the Davidson County Courthouse. Dinner (the noon meal) time at Stamey's surely beat our high school cafeteria fare. After all, we didn't care about nutrition. We craved barbecue. For a dollar or less, we were served a chopped or sliced sandwich and a Coke. We didn't need or want French fries or hushpuppies. Any change we got back was left as a modest tip.

The chopped barbecue was ground medium fine and came sauced from the kitchen. It had brown mixed with lean white meat. There was a good, fresh, smoky flavor, but it was definitely not strong. When sauced with dip at the counter, the combination of the dip, meat and slaw tasted heavenly. If we could afford sliced barbecue, which cost a little more, the meat was tender, not overcooked, and was lightly sauced in the kitchen with what was known as "dip." The dip was reddish-brown and thin, with a good tangy, vinegary and peppery taste. The red slaw was crisp, fresh, moderately finely chopped and slightly vinegary with a hint of pepper.

The '50s high school crowd was not the first to crave Lexington barbecue—not by a long shot. We were simply carrying on a tradition begun in the 1920s when Superior Court sessions were held from two to four weeks per year and were of considerable community significance. Vendors sold refreshments in front of Lawyers' Row, located directly behind the Old Courthouse. There the famous Lexington barbecue had its origin as Sid Weaver prepared, cooked and sold his product in a tent. Jess Swicegood put up a barbecue tent directly across the street from Weaver. These two men would wake up early and gather hickory wood from the forest. They would slow-cook pig shoulders, the cut of choice, for many hours. They would then cover the meat in a tomato-based sauce of vinegar and spices. The aroma would fill the town, and people would flock to get lunch from the tent establishments around the city. Both Weaver and Swicegood later upgraded from tents to small buildings.

When people who have moved away since their high school days during the '50s return to the Piedmont Triad for visits, one of the first meals they want is Lexington barbecue.

STRONG ELEMENTS OF CONSERVATISM

Perhaps one of the things that most characterizes the 1950s was the strong element of conservatism and anticommunist feeling that ran throughout much of society. One of the best indicators of the conservative frame of mind was the addition of the phrase "under God" to the Pledge of Allegiance. Religion was seen as an indicator of anticommunism. Clothing in the '50s was conservative. Men wore gray flannel suits, and women wore dresses with pinched-in waists and high heels. Families worked together, played together and vacationed together at family-themed entertainment areas like national parks. Gender roles were strongly held; girls played with Barbie dolls and Dale Evans gear and boys with Roy Rogers and Davy Crockett paraphernalia.

Fashion successes were Bill Blass and his blue jeans, poodle skirts made of felt and decorated with sequins and poodle appliqués, ponytails for girls and flattops and crew cuts for guys. Saddle shoes and blue suede loafers were popular. Fad hits with kids were toys like hula-hoops, Hopalong Cassidy guns and western gear, Davy Crockett coonskin hats and Silly Putty.

Books and literature reflected the conflict of self-satisfaction and cultural self-doubt about conformity and the true worth of American values. Authors like Norman Vincent Peale, who wrote *The Power of Positive Thinking*, or Bishop Fulton J. Sheen, who penned *Life Is Worth Living*, praised the power of the individual to control his or her fate. The concern with conformity was reflected in David Riesman's *The Lonely Crowd* or Sloan Wilson's *The Man in the Gray Flannel Suit*. A new group of authors appeared on the scene in the form of the beat generation (some called them "beatniks").

Books that defined the time included *The Lonely Crowd* by David Riesman, *Player Piano* by Kurt Vonnegut, *The Power Elite* by C. Wright Mills, *The Bridges at Toko-Ri* by James Michener, *The Conservative Mind* by Russell Kirk, *The Crucial Decade: America 1945–1955* by Eric F. Goldman and *Mrs. Bridge* by Evan Connell.

Children read the Newbery Medal award winners from 1950 through 1959, which included the following books:

- *The Door in the Wall* by Marguerite de Angeli (1950)
- *Amos Fortune, Free Man* by Elizabeth Yates (1951)
- *Ginger Pye* by Eleanor Estes (1952)
- *Secret of the Andes* by Ann Nolan Clark (1953)
- *...And Now Miguel* by Joseph Krumgold (1954)
- *The Wheel on the School* by Meindert DeJong (1955)
- *Carry On, Mr. Bowditch* by Jean Lee Latham (1956)
- *Miracle on Maple Hill* by Virginia Sorenson (1957)
- *Rifles for Watie* by Harold Keith (1958)
- *The Witch of Black Bird Pond* by Elizabeth George Spesare (1959)

The Catcher in the Rye, a 1951 novel by J.D. Salinger, was originally published for adults but became popular with adolescent readers for its themes of teenage confusion, angst, alienation and rebellion. The novel's protagonist and antihero, Holden Caulfield, became an icon for teenage rebellion. It has been challenged in the United States and other countries for its liberal use of profanity and portrayal of sexuality. It also deals with complex issues of identity, belonging, connection and alienation.

TELEPHONE PARTY LINE

Way back when, neighbors did not have private telephone lines. Instead, eight or ten homes in the same area were on the same "party line." When someone picked up his or her phone to dial a number (which was only four digits), that person had to listen closely to make sure that the line was clear. That rarely happened. The correct protocol was to hang up the receiver *immediately.* That rarely happened, too.

It was especially interesting to hear teenagers wooing each other, women talking to their doctors and neighborhood gossipers. Nothing was sacred with a telephone party line. In fact, this seemed to be an amazing source of information. Occasionally, the people being listened in on would notice something strange on the line and yell into the receiver, "Hang up your phone, nosey! You can have the line in ten minutes, but hang up *now*."

Apparently, party line subscribers repeatedly asked for directions on how to ring someone on their line. The following directions were printed and distributed:

> *Set down the number 15. Add the third from the last digit of your own number and then the third from last digit of the number you wish to call (refer to directory for this), and you have the proper four-digit number. Dial this number as formerly, then hang up and let it ring until your party answers.*

Complicated? You bet. It was much more fun to *listen in* than to go through those directions.

WE NEVER LOCKED OUR DOORS UNTIL...

The doors of many homes in the Piedmont Triad were never locked; in fact, during the hot and humid summer nights, the front and back doors were left open so any stray breeze could shift through the wire screen doors. After one incident that left families shaking in their boots, the portals were locked up tight. This is what occurred to bring about fear and trepidation in 1954:

Mrs. Nannie Lanning Doss, 49-year-old grandmother admitted poisoning four of five husbands and was charged with the murder of her mother, Mrs. Lou E. Hazel. A court order was issued to exhume the graves of Mrs. Sarah Elizabeth Lanning, mother-in-law of Mrs. Doss and also Arlie J. Lanning, one of Mrs. Doss' husbands. Bodies were removed from graves of Frank Harrelson, another husband whom Mrs. Doss has admitted poisoning, Robert Lee Higgins, 2, grandson of Mrs. Doss, and Mrs. Dovie Weaver, a sister of Mrs. Doss. Mrs. Doss has denied any responsibility for the death of the Higgins child and Mrs. Weaver.

Not only were our doors firmly secured and windows shut and locked, but we children also slept with our heads under the covers, where we had nightmares about Mrs. Doss and her victims.

CLAIM TO FAME

When twins Dot and Grace Alexander entered High Point College as freshmen, they already had a claim to fame that most young women would envy. When they were seventeen years old, *Time*, *Life* and *Ladies' Home Journal* had featured the Alexander sisters in a full-color Chesterfield cigarette advertisement. The girls appeared in patriotic majorette uniforms, saluting with their right hands and balancing batons under their left armpits. All the while, each girl daintily held a cigarette between her left forefinger and middle finger.

The twins were Chesterfield's "Girls of the Month" and joined ranks with movie stars Betty Grable, Rita Hayworth, Claudette Colbert, Dorothy Lamour and Rosalind Russell.

Do You Remember These?

Above: When beauty rituals were necessary daily occurrences? *Courtesy of author.*

Right: Beanie caps that made you look like something from outer space? *Courtesy of author.*

Epilogue

Fun to Remember, but Wow, I'm Old

This following interesting tidbit of remembrance was e-mailed to the author of this book by her "best-est friend" in the '50s and '60s (and still today), Sarah Gibson Andrews. It's an appropriate (and true) close to this book about growing up in the Piedmont Triad of North Carolina:

Someone Asked the Other Day, "What was your favorite fast food when you were growing up?"

"We didn't have fast food when I was growing up," I informed him. "All the food was slow."

"C'mon, seriously. Where did you eat?"

By this time, the kid was laughing so hard I was afraid he was going to suffer serious internal damage, so I didn't tell him the part about how I had to have permission to leave the table.

But here are some other things I would have told him about my childhood if I figured his system could have handled it.

"I was 21 before I tasted my first pizza; it was called 'pizza pie.' When I bit into it, I burned the roof of my mouth and the cheese slid off, swung down, plastered itself against my chin and burned that, too. It's still the best pizza I ever had."

"I never had a telephone in my room. The only phone in the house was in the living room, and it was on a party line. Before you could dial, you had to listen and make sure some people you didn't know weren't already using the line."

Then there are those true, tricky "Do You Remember" incidents, such as the ones here:

My Dad was cleaning out my grandmother's house, and he brought me an old Royal Crown Cola bottle. In the bottle top was a stopper with a bunch of holes in it. I knew immediately what it was, but my daughter had no idea. She thought they had tried to make it a salt shaker or something. I knew it as the bottle that sat on the end of the ironing board to "sprinkle" clothes with because we didn't have steam irons.

So, how many do you remember?

- headlight dimmer switches on the floor
- ignition switches on the dashboard
- heaters mounted on the inside of the fire wall
- real iceboxes
- pant leg clips for bicycles without chain guards
- soldering irons you heat on a gas burner
- using hand signals for cars without turn signals

Ready for an "Older than Dirt" quiz? Count all the ones that you remember, not the ones you were told about. Ratings are at the bottom:

- Blackjack chewing gum
- wax Coke-shaped bottles with colored sugar water
- candy cigarettes
- soda pop machines that dispensed glass bottles
- coffee shops or diners with tableside juke boxes
- home milk delivery in glass bottles with cardboard stoppers
- party lines on the telephone
- newsreels before the movie
- P.F. Flyers
- Butch wax

- TV test patterns that came on at night after the last show and were there until TV shows started again in the morning; there were only three channels (if you were fortunate)
- peashooters
- Howdy Doody
- 45 RPM records
- S&H Green Stamps
- hi-fi's
- metal ice trays with levers
- mimeograph paper
- blue flashbulb
- Packards
- roller-skate keys
- cork popguns
- drive-ins
- Studebakers
- washtub wringers

If you remember 0–5, "You're still young."
If you remember 6–10, "You're getting older."
If you remember 11–15, "Don't tell your age."
If you remember 16–25, "You're older than dirt!"

Egads. I'm older than dirt, but those memories are some of the best parts of my life.

Tried and True Recipes from the Good Ol' Piedmont Triad Days

Tuna Noodle Casserole

6 ounces long noodles
1 can condensed mushroom soup
1 cup milk
1 7-ounce can tuna fish
¼ pound processed yellow cheese (finely diced or coarsely grated)

Cook noodles in large amount of salted boiling water until tender; drain. Stir soup and milk together in baking dish. Add noodles, tuna and cheese; stir gently to mix. Bake at 375 degrees F for 25 to 30 minutes. Yields 4 servings.

Barbecue Sauce for Spare Ribs

To make a sauce for barbecued spare ribs, combine a quarter cup of cider vinegar, a half cup of savory bottled thick brown sauce (the kind usually used as an accompaniment for cold meat or steak), one and a half teaspoons of salt and two teaspoons of prepared mustard. Pour the liquid mixture over ribs and bake in a moderate oven for about an hour and a half. Baste frequently with the sauce, adding a little water at the end of the roasting time if necessary.

CORNMEAL GRIDDLE CAKES

1 cup cornmeal
1 cup all-purpose flour
1 teaspoon salt
4 teaspoons baking powder
1 egg, well beaten
2½ cups milk
¼ cup shortening, melted

Mix dry ingredients; combine egg and milk and stir in the mixed dry ingredients. Stir in the shortening and add more milk if necessary to make a thick batter. Fry on a hot greased griddle.

CHICKEN FRIED STEAK

2 pounds beef bottom round, trimmed of excess fat
2 teaspoons kosher salt
1 teaspoon freshly ground black pepper
1 cup all-purpose flour
3 whole eggs, beaten
¼ cup vegetable oil
2 cups chicken broth
½ cup whole milk
½ teaspoon fresh thyme leaves

Preheat oven to 250 degrees F.

Cut the meat with the grain into half-inch-thick slices. Season each piece on both sides with the salt and pepper. Place the flour into a pie pan. Place the eggs into a separate pie pan. Dredge the meat on both sides in the flour. Tenderize the meat, using a kneading device, until each slice is a fourth of an inch thick. Once tenderized, dredge the meat again in the flour, followed by the egg and, finally, back in the flour again. Repeat with all the pieces of meat. Place the meat onto a plate and allow it to sit for 10 to 15 minutes before cooking.

Place enough of the vegetable oil to cover the bottom of a twelve-inch slope-sided skillet and set over medium-high heat. Once the oil begins to shimmer, add the meat in batches, being careful not to overcrowd the pan. Cook each piece on both sides until golden brown, approximately 4 minutes per side. Remove the steaks to a wire rack set in a half sheet pan and place into the oven. Repeat until all of the meat is browned.

Add the remaining vegetable oil, or at least 1 tablespoon, to the pan. Whisk in 3 tablespoons of the flour left over from the dredging. Add the chicken broth and deglaze the pan. Whisk until the gravy comes to a boil and begins to thicken. Add the milk and thyme and whisk until the gravy coats the back of a spoon, approximately 5 to 10 minutes. Season to taste with more salt and pepper, if needed. Serve the gravy over the steaks.

SPECIAL FLOUNDER FILLETS

small or ½ onion, chopped
olive oil
1 egg
¾ cup bread crumbs
½ cup grated Parmesan cheese
garlic powder, salt and pepper
2 pounds flounder fillets

Place the onion in a frying pan with enough olive oil to sauté it. Whisk the egg in a bowl. Combine the breadcrumbs, cheese and a dash each of the seasonings. Coat fish with egg and roll through crumb mixture. Increase the temperature in the frying pan to medium high and fry the fish quickly with the sautéed onions, adding a little more olive oil if necessary. Don't overcook; fish is done when it flakes with a fork. Serve with cocktail sauce on the side. Serves 4.

OVEN BAKED FLOUNDER

½ teaspoon garlic powder
½ teaspoon oregano

dash of salt and pepper
1 cup bread crumbs
2 pounds of thick flounder fillets
2 cups milk
⅓ cup butter, melted

Preheat oven to 500 degrees F. Add garlic, oregano, salt and pepper to breadcrumbs. Dip fillets in milk and roll in crumb mixture. Place on greased baking sheet and drizzle with butter. Bake for 10 to 12 minutes. Serves 4 to 5.

COUNTRY HAM AND RED-EYE GRAVY

Start the ham slices in a cold skillet over low to medium heat. "Fried" ham is practically a misnomer; you are little more than sweating the meat, five minutes per side. After you have removed the meat from the skillet, add ¼ to ½ cup of water, depending on how much in the way of pan juices you have. Stir, scraping up any bits in the pan. Cover and cook for two or three minutes. Uncover the pan and boil the gravy briefly to reduce it. It will not be thick, and there isn't much of it.

There is a variation that uses coffee instead of water. Think of red-eye as poor man's sauce—pan juices eked out with what was at hand, and it was either free water or cheap leftover coffee.

PULLED PORK

2 cups cider vinegar
¼ cup packed brown sugar
1 tablespoon red pepper flakes
1 tablespoon Worcestershire sauce
1 teaspoon salt
hot pepper sauce, to taste
4 cups wood chips (use hickory or oak chips for the best flavor)
1 5- to 5½-pound boneless pork shoulder roast
10 to 12 hamburger buns, split and toasted
coleslaw (optional)

BARBECUE SAUCE: In medium bowl, combine vinegar, brown sugar, red pepper flakes, Worcestershire sauce, salt and hot pepper sauce. Divide sauce into two portions; set aside.

PULLED PORK: At least 1 hour before grilling, soak wood chips in enough water to cover; drain before using. Rub meat with salt and black pepper. In a charcoal grill with a cover, place preheated coals around a drip pan for medium indirect heat. Add half an inch of hot water to drip pan. Sprinkle half of the drained wood chips over the coals. Place meat on grill rack over drip pan. Cover and grill about 4 hours or until meat is very tender. Add more preheated coals (use a hibachi or a metal chimney starter to preheat coals), wood chips and hot water every 1 to 1½ hours. Remove meat from grill; cover with foil and let stand for 20 to 30 minutes. Using a fork, shred meat into long, thin strands. Pour sauce over shredded meat; toss to coat. Serve on toasted buns. If desired, top meat with coleslaw. Serve remaining sauce on the side. Serves 10 to 12. Note: For gas grills, preheat and then turn off any burners directly below where the food will go. The heat circulates inside the grill, so turning the food is not necessary.

HOT AND CHEESY CHICKEN CASSEROLE

Optimistic tasty dinner "without walls."

3 cups chopped cooked chicken
14-ounce package frozen broccoli florets
2 cups cooked rice
1½ cups frozen peas
1 10.75-ounce can condensed cream of chicken soup
1 10.75-ounce can condensed fiesta nacho cheese soup
1 10–10.5-ounce can diced tomatoes and green chili peppers
½ cup milk
½ teaspoon crushed red pepper (optional)
½ cup shredded cheddar cheese (2 ounces)
½ cup shredded mozzarella cheese (2 ounces)
1 cup crushed rich round crackers

Preheat oven to 350 degrees F. Place chicken in bottom of a 13x9x2-inch baking dish or 3-quart rectangular casserole. In large bowl, combine broccoli, rice and peas. Spread mixture over the chicken. In medium bowl, combine cream of chicken soup, nacho cheese soup, diced tomatoes, milk and crushed red pepper. Stir in ¼ cup of the cheddar cheese and ¼ cup of the mozzarella cheese. Pour mixture over broccoli mixture in baking dish. Sprinkle crushed crackers evenly over all. Top with remaining cheddar and mozzarella cheeses.

Famous Skeen Burgers

Exactly as the recipe says, passed down from generation to generation.

To make a Skeen Burger, start with 5 pounds of fresh ground chuck. The fresher the better, and make sure it has some fat in it—none of that 95-5 stuff. Crush enough Ritz Crackers to make 1 cup of cracker crumbs. Have on hand 1 cup of good apple sauce, 3 tsp. of Tabasco sauce, 5 tbsp. of Worcestershire sauce (spring for the good stuff of your choice; leave the French's for the kiddies), 1 envelope of dry onion soup mix, ½ tsp. garlic powder and salt if you wish—sea salt works best.

Mix it all up in whatever order you wish in one big bowl using your hands. Machines destroy the texture of the meat. Pat out into generous burgers—we usually get 13–15 or so from this recipe. Be careful about getting them too thick as they tend to plump up as you grill them.

Yes, grill them—over charcoal. Be sure it is fairly hot, and sear the first side—some black does not hurt the taste—I think it enhances it. Flip them over and sear the other side. Flip again for 2–3 minutes, then flip for another 2–3. Use your turner to press them down on the grill and watch how much juice comes out. When it stops coming out in a stream, but the outside of the burgers are still moist, they're done. Cooked like this they are usually medium to medium well.

Get them off the grill and then use the grill to toast the buns. Onion, tomato, lettuce, ketchup and whatever else you want on a burger, including chili (no beans—hot dog chili). Sweet tea to wash them down, although beer will do as well. Chips, if you wish, potato salad works well, and homemade ice cream for after is just the thing.

Bibliography

About.com. "History of the Electric Blanket." http://inventors.about.com/od/estartinventions/a/ElectricBlanket.htm.

———. "The Twist." http://history1900.about.com/od/1960/qt.Twist.htm.

BBQ in Lexington, NC. "BBQ: Then and Now." http://agbritt.com/BBQ/BBQThenNow.html.

Beauty Parlor 212. "1950s Housewife Era and Rock and Roll Inspired Makeup Trends and Vintage Fashion Styles." http://beautyparlor212.blogspot.com/2010/12/1950s-housewife-era-and-rock-and-roll.html.

Betty Crocker. "Polls, Quizzes and Betty Crocker History." http://www.bettycrocker.com/community/forums/17/32621.

BookRags. "Dime Stores/Woolworth's." http://www.bookrags.com/history/dime-storeswoolworths-sjpc-01.

Brinkley Walser. "The Law & Lexington Barbecue." http://www.brinkleywalser.com/firm_history/law.html.

Byerly, Victoria. *Hard Times Cotton Mill Girls: Personal Histories of Womanhood and Poverty in the South.* New York: Cornell University ILR Press, New York State School of Industrial and Labor Relations, 1986.

Candy Warehouse. "Black Jack Gum." http://www.candywarehouse.com/products/black-jack-gum-5-stick-packs-20-piece-box.

City of Winston-Salem, NC. "Events Mark 50th Anniversary of the First Sit-in Victory." http://www.cityofws.org/Home/Departments/MarketingAndCommunications/NewsArchive/News2010/Articles/EventsMark50thAnniversaryOfTheFirstSit-inVictory.

Crazed Fanboy. http://www.crazedfanboy.com/npcr11/s-h-green-stamps.php.

Daniels, Elayne Salzber, and Joan C. Chrisler. "Beauty Is the Beast: Psychological Effects of the Pursuit of the Perfect Female Body." In *Women: A Feminist Perspective.* Fifty Edition. Edited by Jo Freeman. Mountain View, CA: Mayfield Publishing Company, 1995.

The Department Store Museum. "Thalhimer Brothers, Richmond, Virginia." http://departmentstoremuseum.blogspot.com/2010/11/thalhimer-brothers-richmond-virginia.html.

ElderWeb. "Home Care Drops in Popularity, 1950–1959." http://www.elderweb.com/book/export/html/2846.

Elvis Concerts. "Elvis Presley in Concert." http://www.elvisconcerts.com/newspapers/press161.htm.

———. "Elvis Presley to Play Here." http://www.elvisconcerts.com/newspapers/a56031201.jpg.

Fox Movietone News. "A History of the Newsreel." http://www.movietonews.com/the_fox_movietone_newsreel.html.

Foy, Missy. Oral history interview with Edith Mayfield Wiggins, May 8, 1991.

The Freeholder. "Skeen Burgers." http://thefreehold.blogspot.com/2009/01/skeen-burgers.html.

Greensboro Daily Photo. "The Polio Children's Hospital of Greensboro." http://www.greensborodailyphoto.com/2009/06/the-polio-hospital.html.

Hagan, Tere. *Sterling Flatware: An Identification and Value Guide.* Gate City, IN: L-W Book Sales, 1999.

Hamid Circus Inc. "George A. Hamid Sr." http://hamidcircus.com/about/ghamidsr.html.

International Lyrics Playground. "What It Was, Was Football." http://lyricsplayground.com/alpha/songs/w/whatitwaswasfootball.shtml.

Internet Archive. "Universal Newsreels." http://archive.org/details/universal_newsreels.

Interview by author of Estie Culler Bennington, June 21, 2012.

[Lexington, NC] *Dispatch.* "Ann Southern to Leave TV for New Film with Lucille Ball." October 30, 1957.

———. "Another Dispersal Item." January 14, 1954.

———. "Another Honor Goes to Miss Piedmont Queen." December 4, 1958.

———. "Another Postal Problem Is Moving Writing Table." July 15, 1948.

———. "The Balfour." December 19, 1952.

———. "Betty Jo Ring Urges Young Ladies Over State to Enter N.C. Pageant." January 26, 1955.

———. "Big Annual Fair at Winston-Salem During Next Week." September 28, 1948.

———. "Canned Foods Advice Given for the Fair." September 24, 1953.

———. "Chamber of Commerce Plans Industrial Exhibit at Fair." September 24, 1953.

———. "Coloring Contest Rules." December 6, 1954.

———. "Conflicting Stories Told: Negro Boy Shot by White Youth." December 6, 1954.

———. "Craver Reunion Will Be Held at Arcadia on September 2." August 30, 1951.

———. "Dancers Perform for the Civitans." October 27, 1948.

———. "Drug Store Advertisement." May 3, 1945.

———. "Egg Breaking Plant to Open Early February." January 15, 1950.

———. "Elvis Seen as Way to Educate Public on Sex." August 1, 1956.

———. "Erlanger to Have Halloween Fete." October 27, 1948.

———. "Farmers Pleased at Weather, Says Bethany Writer." November 5, 1948.

———. "Fine Law Point Frees Defendant in County Court." April 29, 1948.

———. "Greater Greensboro Open with Ford and Snead Leading." April 11, 1957.

———. "Greensboro Negroes Plan More Marches." May 27, 1963.

———. "Hargrave Heads Gas Rationing for District: Registration in All the Grammar Schools of County Next Week." May 7, 1942.

———. "Hollywood." October 27, 1948.

———. "Home City Will Honor Dick Walser Thursday." April 29, 1948.

———. "Junior-Senior Prom and Banquet Friday." May 17, 1945.

———. "Madame Avant: American Palmist and Advisor." April 29, 1948.

———. Mann's Drug Advertisements. April 2, 1953.

———. "Ministers Hit Sunday Movies in Thomasville." July 25, 1951.

———. "Mrs. Conrad Speaker at W.C.T.U. Meeting." May 17, 1945.

———. "New Juliet Lowe Stamps." December 6, 1954.

———. "Open Forum." December 19, 1952.

———. "Plummer Goes to Greensboro in Effort to Procure Order: Sheriff Cox to Sign Second Warrant for Murder by Poison." December 6, 1954.

———. "Problem of Reconstruction: Here Today for Discussions with Property Owners; Part of Walls May Be Saved; Brockwell Will Inspect." December 6, 1945.

———. "A Protest Against Dumping." September 5, 1956.

———. "Publishing House Hints Facts on Flying Saucers: Says in School Paper that Saucers Belong to U.S. Air Force." September 30, 1950.

———. "Repeat: How to Ring Number on Your Own Line." February 17, 1950.

———. "Seven High School Juniors to Attend Tar Heel Girls' State." May 17, 1945.

———. "Social and Civic Events." November 5, 1948.

———. "Social Life at Midway Lively." November 5, 1948.

———. "Southmont, Linwood Halloween Affairs." October 27, 1948.

———. "Suggestions for Christmas Mail Listed by Postmaster." December 6, 1954.

———. "Tell Her She Looks Well and Strong." May 3, 1945.

———. "Textile Night Slated; McCree Winning Pitcher." August 30, 1951.

———. "Three More Polio Cases Are Reported in Davidson County." July 15, 1948.

———. "Tom Thumb Wedding at Cecil Tuesday." May 17, 1945.

———. "Trinity W.S.C.S. Meets with Mrs. Michael." May 17, 1945.

———. "Two More School Bomb Hoaxes Reported." December 8, 1958.

———. "Word Is Going Around Whereby Talebearers and Gossipers that Evangelist Charles A. Keyes, Jr., Steals Organ During Revival at County Courthouse." October 27, 1948.

Long Star College—Kingwood. "American Cultural History 1950–1959." http://kclibrary.lonestar.edu/decade50.html.

News Record. "Survivor Shares Her Strength." October 7, 2007.

———. "Woman Who Spent 61 Years in Iron Lung Dies." August 9, 2012.

North Carolina Barbecue Company. "Founding Fathers of North Carolina Barbecue." http://ncbbqcompany.com/blog/2011/06/15/founding-fathers-of-north-carolina-barbecue.

North Carolina Barbecue Society. "Stamey's Barbecue, Greensboro." http://www.ncbbqsociety.com/trail_pages/stameys_large.html.

Old Time Candy. http://www.oldtimecandy.com/candylist.htm.

Pett, Saul. "Want to Cry a Little? Look at TV Soap Opera." *Dispatch*, May 5, 1955.

Priddy's General Store. http://www.priddysgeneralstore.com.

Railey, John. "Opinion." *Winston-Salem Journal*, May 22, 2011.

Readex Blog. "Posts Tagged 'Women's Society of Christian Service.'" http://blog.readex.com/tag/womens-society-of-christian-service.

Retro Housewife. "Beauty and Cosmetics in the 1950s." http://www.retro-housewife.com/1950-beauty-and-cosmetics.html.

Scearce, Flora Ann. *Cotton Mill Girl.* Mustang, OK: Tate Publishing & Enterprises, 2006.

Sexton, Scott. "Danbury General Store Is a Slice of the Real Thing." *Winston-Salem Journal*, September 4, 2012.

Shapard, Robert P. Oral history interview with Edith Mayfield Wiggins, October 24, 2006.

Sherrow, Victoria. *Encyclopedia of Hair: A Culture History.* Westport, CT: Greenwood Publishing Group, 2006.

Sink, Alice E. *The Great Crippler and Polio Heroes.* Kernersville, NC: Alabaster Publishing, 2011.

ST Lyrics. "The Twist." http://www.stlyrics.com/lyrics/heartsinatlantis/thetwist.htm.

Tar Heel Girls State. http://www.thgs.com/index.htm.

———. "THGS Dress Code." http://www.thgs.com/thgs_dress_code.htm.

Time. "Top 10 Things Today's Kids Will Never Experience." http://www.time.com/time/specials/packages/completelist/0,29569,2011482,00.html.

Tomlin, Jimmy. "Strike Up the Brand: 'Chesterfield Twins' Shared Spotlight in Early 1940s." *High Point Enterprise*, September 9, 2012.

The White House. "Dwight D. Eisenhower." http://www.whitehouse.gov/about/presidents/dwightdeisenhower.

Wiki Answers. "What Is a Newsreel?" http://wiki.answers.com/Q/What_is_a_newsreel.

Wikipedia. "The Andy Griffith Show." http://en.wikipedia.org/wiki/The_Andy_Griffith_Show.

———. "Bowman Gray Stadium." http://en.wikipedia.org/wiki/Bowman_Gray_Stadium.

———. "The Catcher in the Rye." http://en.wikipedia.org/wiki/The+Catcher_in_the_Rye.

———. "First Inauguration of Dwight D. Eisenhower." http://en.wikipedia.org/wiki/First_inauguration_of_Dwight_D._Eisenhower.

———. "Frances Willard (suffragist)." http://en.wikipedia.org/wiki/Frances_Willard_(suffragist).

———. "The Garry Moore Show." http://en.wikipedia.org/wiki/The_Garry_Moore_Show.

———. "General Tom Thumb." http://en.wikipedia.org/wiki/General_Tom_Thumb.

———. "George Rice 'Joie' Chitwood." http://en.wikipedia.org/wiki/Joie_Chitwood.

———. "Glamour Photography." http://en.wikipedia.org/wiki/Glamour_photography.

———. "Groucho Marx." http://en.wikipedia.org/wiki/Groucho_Marx.

———. "Hopscotch." http://en.wikipedia.org/wiki/Hopscotch.

———. "Krispy Kreme." http://en.wikipedia.org/wiki/Krispy_Kreme.

———. "Mary Kay and Johnny." http://en.wikipedia.org/wiki/Mary_Kay_and_Johnny.

———. "Minstrel Show." http://en.wikipedia.org/wiki/Minstrel_show.

———. "The Paleface (1948 film)." http://en.wikipedia.org/wiki/The_Paleface_(1948_film).

———. "Palmistry." http://en.wikipedia.org/wiki/Palmistry.

———. "Piedmont Triad." http://en.wikipedia.org/wiki/Piedmont_Triad.

———. "Poorhouse." http://en.wikipedia.org/wiki/Poorhouse.

———. "Rexall." http://en.wikipedia.org/wiki/Rexall.

———. "Search for Tomorrow." http://en.wikipedia.org/wiki/Search_for_Tomorrow.

———. "S&H Green Stamps." http://en.wikipedia.org/wiki/S%26H_Green_Stamps.

———. "S.H. Kress & Co." http://en.wikipedia.org/wiki/S._H._Kress_%26_Co.

———. "Stock Car Racing." http://en.wikipedia.org/wiki/Stock_car_racing.

———. "This Is My Song." http://en.wikipedia.org/wiki/This_Is_My_Song_(1934_song).

———. "Woman's Christian Temperance Union." http://en.wikipedia.org/wiki/Woman's_Christian_Temperance_Union.

———. "Written on the Wind." http://en.wikipedia.org/wiki/Written_on_the_Wind.

Yes! Weekly. "1948 Polio Epidemic." http://www.yesweekly.com/triad/article-4702-1948-polio-epidemic.html.

About the Author

Alice E. Sink is the published author of numerous nonfiction and fiction books, short stories, articles and essays. She earned her master's of fine arts degree in creative writing from the University of North Carolina–Greensboro. For thirty years, she taught writing courses at High Point University in High Point, North Carolina, where she received the Meredith Clark Slane Distinguished Teaching/Service Award in 2002. The North Carolina Arts Council and the partnering arts councils of the Central Piedmont Regional Artists Hub Program awarded Sink a 2007 grant to promote her writing. She lives in Kernersville, North Carolina, with her husband, Tom, and their rescued dogs and cats.

www.ingramcontent.com/pod-product-compliance
Lightning Source LLC
Chambersburg PA
CBHW070924150426
42812CB00049B/1487